Cambridge Topics in Geography: second series

Editors   Alan R. H. Baker, Emmanuel College, Cambridge
Colin Evans, King's College School, Wimbledon

Coasts

J. D. Hansom
University of Sheffield

Cambridge University Press

Cambridge
New York   New Rochelle   Melbourne   Sydney

For Shelagh, Donald and Stuart

Published by the Press Syndicate of the University of Cambridge
The Pitt Building, Trumpington Street, Cambridge CB2 1RP
32 East 57th Street, New York, NY 10022, USA
10 Stamford Road, Oakleigh, Melbourne 3166, Australia

First published 1988

Printed in Great Britain at the University Press, Cambridge

British Library cataloguing in publication data

Hansom, J.D.
  Coasts
  I. Title
  551.4'57

Library of Congress cataloguing in publication data

Hansom, J.D.
  Coasts/J.D. Hansom.
  p. cm. – (Cambridge topics in geography. Second series)
  Bibliography: p.
  Includes index.
  1. Coasts.   I. Title.   II. Series
  GB451.2.H36 1988   88–15966
  551.4'57 – dc19   CIP

ISBN 0 521 30911 5 hard covers
ISBN 0 521 31377 5 paperback

DS

Contents

Preface

There can be few places more uncomfortable or sights more awe-inspiring than the wave-torn coastline during a severe storm. Yet when the sea is glassy calm and sunshine bathes the beach, the coast reveals a more benign face. Perhaps it is as much this contrast as the incredibly varied nature of the coast that makes it an attractive subject for the geographer. General interest in the coast, its forms and its processes, is also increasing in response to an accelerating use of coastal land. Knowledge of the coastal system is essential for efficient and wise use of the coastal resource.

This book aims to provide an introduction to the physical nature of the coastal environment by examining coastal processes and landforms at a level that is easily accessible to both A-level students and first-year undergraduates studying coasts as part of a more general course. It is intended to bridge the gap between the superficial level of general texts and the more detailed presentation in advanced texts and research papers. Such a background in processes and forms is necessary to allow students to tackle adequately the applied issues of erosion and coastal zone management that are increasingly themes in both A-level geography and undergraduate courses.

Building from a discussion of the elements of the coast and of the factors affecting them, the book examines the processes and forms of rocky coasts before outlining the depositional environments of beaches and related forms, sand dunes and estuaries. The influence of sea-level change adds a temporal perspective whereas the current state of the coast is treated in an overview in Chapter 8, People and coasts, which deals with human-induced erosion, pollution and coastal problems. The book draws mainly on coastal examples in the British Isles but where appropriate, examples from coasts worldwide have been used; mangroves are in scarce supply around British coasts!

I am most grateful to the editors of the series for useful comments on the manuscript; to Professor Alan Hay for the generous use of the office, cartographic and photographic facilities in the Department of Geography at Sheffield; to Paul Coles for transforming my thumbnail sketches into respectable diagrams; and to Joan Dunn, Margaret Gray and Jean Walters for typing the manuscript.

Jim Hansom
University of Sheffield

1 Introduction

Why study coasts?

In the low countries of Europe, serious coastal flooding was reported
for the years 1014, 1099, 1170, 1175, 1225, 1277, 1285, 1288, 1323, 1337,
1357, 1377, 1404, 1421, 1468, 1526, 1530, 1532, 1551, 1570, and so on,
and in England for the years . . . 1949, 1953, 1976, 1978 . . . . The
flood of 1421 is said to have destroyed perhaps as many as 72 villages,
killing between 10,000 and 100,000 people. The 1953 storm killed 307
people in England and destroyed 24,000 houses; in the same storm
1,800 people in the Netherlands lost their lives. On the Suffolk coast,
the cliffs at Covehithe were cut back by 10.7 m in two hours. In 1978,
the piers of Skegness, Hunstanton, Herne Bay and Margate in England
were all destroyed by a storm, thousands of houses were flooded and at
Wells in Norfolk, a 300-tonne coaster was lifted onto the quay! From
this brief and limited survey, it appears that we cannot afford to ignore
the coast and its processes. A classic example of such ignorance was
Julius Caesar, who, unaware of the large tides around the British Isles,
lost several ships and sustained damage to most of his Roman fleet on
an overnight high tide on the coast of southern England.

An understanding of the forces and processes that give rise to such
catastrophic events is of clear advantage to humans for it allows steps to
be taken to minimise or avoid their worst effects. A similar
understanding of the effects of more frequent events of lesser
magnitude is also of great use to all coastal dwellers. Waves and
currents incessantly shift sediment on the coast. During fair weather
and in sheltered locations much of this sediment is deposited and the
coast builds out slightly. During stormy weather and in exposed
locations some of the sediment is removed and the shore erodes. Over
the years if such a coastal location receives more sediment than it loses,
then it moves slowly seawards, building a large coastal plain; the
process is accelerated if sea-level is slowly falling. Conversely a
continued loss of sediment from an area leads to coastal erosion. The
coastal margin is therefore highly variable, its position depending upon
a variety of factors ranging from wave conditions to sediment supply
and sea-level change. Yet people also live on the coast and for centuries
they have gathered food from the shoreline and coastal sea, settled in
coastal towns, traded with others on distant coasts with vessels out of
coastal ports and, increasingly, used the flat land of the coast for the
sites of cities and industries. The variability of the coastal environment
has occasionally made life difficult: blown sands inundated the Stone
Age village of Skara Brae in Orkney, 4,500 years ago; once-prosperous
coastal ports like Chester on the Dee in Cheshire have declined owing
to sediment deposition, as did Rye in Sussex on the south coast of
England. On the other hand, towns such as Hastings in Sussex, Great
Yarmouth and Cromer in Norfolk, and Blackpool in Lancashire all

Fig. 1.1 A sloping seawall and groynes in Aberdeen Bay, Grampian now fixes a previously mobile coast of beach and sand dune. As with many seawalls in the British Isles, a roadway and promenade has been built on top.

have histories of coastal erosion. Few towns or ports on the British coast are not adorned with seawalls or groynes to help fix the position of a shoreline that is inherently variable (Fig. 1.1). The success or failure of these seawalls or other protection devices rests in large part on an understanding of how the coast reacts to changing conditions. As coastal study has increased in quality and quantity over the years, there has been an acceptance that the most satisfactory protection is a wide, flexible beach or, if this is inappropriate, a structure which emulates a beach surface such as a sloping, permeable ramp of boulders or boulder-filled cages (gabions). Armed with such information, coastal authorities are better placed to tackle erosion of the coast.

There is no doubt that coastal erosion and its alleviation must benefit from better coastal knowledge, yet it is important to see the coastal environment in its entirety. Issues of coastal erosion are not divorced from increasing use of coastal land, especially if the protection measures adopted serve to increase erosion elsewhere by adversely affecting coastal processes. Similarly, expansion of houses and factories on the coast have increased use of the coast as a dumping ground for waste, and inadequate knowledge of tidal currents has resulted in unacceptable levels of pollution on many beaches that are valued for recreational purposes (Fig. 1.2). The health risks to humans swimming in these waters are real, as is the plight of many coastal plants and animals whose existence is under threat by accidental or deliberate pollution, e.g. by oil spills, thermal and radioactive wastes and the dumping at sea of toxic chemicals.

Habitats are also under pressure from human expansion into sand dunes, mudflats and salt marshes. Estuaries are particularly at risk, natural deposition producing extensive flat wetland areas that are ideal for reclamation at a fraction of the cost of engineering a similar gain. Once developed, the now largely artificially banked estuary often becomes environmentally degraded because of effluent discharged into its altered tidal currents and assorted household and industrial dumping along its shores.

The coastline comprises a variety of different facets, from the cliffs and beaches of the exposed sea coast to the mudflats and salt marshes of

a

b

c

d

Fig. 1.2 Every coastal land use places some demand on coastal space which may conflict with alternative uses: (a) urban development for tourist use, Mar Menor, Spain; (b) beaches for recreational use, near Marseilles, France; (c) reclamation of coastal wetlands for industrial development, Hong Kong; (d) extraction of beach sediment for coastal engineering use, Rosslare, Co. Wexford, Ireland.

the sheltered estuaries. In each of these environments, the landforms, vegetation and animal populations are subject to processes and pressures that must be understood before we can judge the present state of the environment or predict how it might change in the future. More importantly, we need to know how the coastal environment might alter in response to human manipulation in the form of coastal reclamation, sand dune and earth-cliff rehabilitation and artificial beach nourishment or protection. If we value the coast as an economic as well as a recreational asset, then we must study it.

The coastal system

All coasts are subject to inputs of energy and materials which interact within the geological framework to produce coastal landforms (Fig. 1.3). The energy inputs are provided mainly by waves, tides and

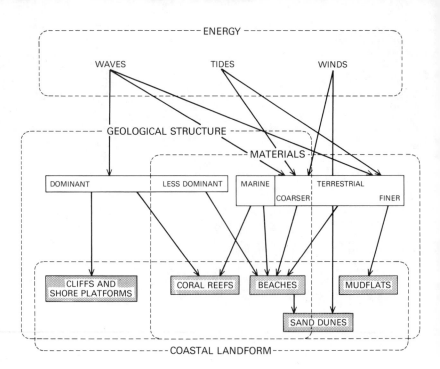

Fig. 1.3 The coastal system.

winds and although the ultimate source of wind and wave energy is the sun, the moon is the principal source of tidal energy. Coastal sediments are built up from several sources: from the materials deposited by rivers or glaciers where they reach the sea; as a result of erosion of the land by waves; from biological production in the seas by coral-type animals; and from pre-existing offshore sediment banks. The geological structure within which the energy and materials interact is the most stable of the main inputs yet in some circumstances it too is subject to change, for example during tectonic faulting or volcanic activity. Coastal processes such as abrasion and quarrying of rocks, nearshore sediment movement and mudflat deposition translate the inputs of energy and materials into the outputs of the coastal system: landforms. The characteristic of the landform depends on the particular combination of inputs and processes acting upon it. For example, a beach subject to incessant stormy conditions may well be coarse-grained with a wide up-beach parabolic profile due to the sweep of stormwave uprush. Coastal landforms that are well adjusted to the present combination of processes acting on them are said to be in *dynamic equilibrium*, meaning that small changes in one input source are accommodated by small reactive changes elsewhere. Thus coastal sand dunes grow in height until they extend into the zone of higher wind velocities where a balance is reached so that the amount of sand deposited exactly equals that eroded by the wind. Beach gradients adjust to accommodate the type of wave breaking on the beach. However, in time there may be major changes to the combination of the inputs due to climatic change, glaciation or sea-level change, for example. Climatic change may alter the energy input via increasing storminess; glaciation may inundate the coast giving rise to glacial rather than coastal features where the valleys are occupied by ice, and to icebergs, seasonal sea-ice and frost-shattering processes on the adjacent coast. Major changes are brought about by sea-level change. Waves and tides vary owing to altered water depths, sediment supply varies because of differing availability of seabed

Fig. 1.4(a)   The plunging cliffs of Moher, Co. Clare, Ireland are composed of horizontally bedded shales which erode to produce vertical faces. Change on such a rock coast may be extremely slow and may span several changes in sea-level.

(b)   The overdeepened trough of Aurlandsfjord, Norway is related to past glacial processes rather than to the marine processes operating today.

a

b

sediment, and the geological structure varies because the coastline itself may have been moved considerable distances inland if sea-level has risen and offshore if sea-level has fallen.

Sea-levels have changed greatly over the last million years, and especially in the last 35,000 years the changes have fundamentally affected the coastal landforms that we see today. Most depositional features like beaches and salt marshes are sensitive to sea-level change and quickly adjust to the new conditions, adapting their form if the change in sea-level is gradual and abandoning old forms to develop new ones if the change is large and rapid. Rocky coasts, especially high and steep ones, adjust very slowly to changes and many of our present cliffs owe their form to past sea-levels having been only superficially modified by processes at present sea-level. The concept of coastal landforms adjusting towards equilibrium with inputs and thus with processes is important since it highlights the point that some landforms react virtually instantaneously to change, whereas others react on a timescale that may be greater than the duration of the changed conditions themselves. These landforms may rarely, if ever, be in equilibrium with the processes operating on them (Fig. 1.4 a,b).

Coastal nomenclature

The coast can be subdivided seawards in terms of wave process zones (Fig. 1.5):

1 The *offshore zone* comprises water of depths greater than half the wave length of the incoming waves. Wave-induced sediment movement is limited since for most practical purposes substantial sediment movement occurs only in water shallower than about 20 m.
2 The *nearshore zone* is the area in which most modification to waves and virtually all the sediment movement occurs. Consequently it is the most important of the coastal zones. It extends from the limit of the offshore zone to the limit of wave influence on the beach. Within the nearshore zone are several other zones:
   (a) The most seaward area is the *breaker zone* where breaking waves occur. Since wave-breaking depends on the characteristics of the waves, the breaker zone is variable in extent.
   (b) The zone occupied by broken waves travelling towards the shore is the *surf zone*. Most of the sediment moved by waves on and offshore as well as alongshore by oblique waves occurs in this zone.
   (c) The most landward area of the nearshore zone is the *swash zone*. This is the area of the shore that is alternately covered by the swash or wave uprush and exposed by the backwash as the wave recedes. The extent and location of the swash zone changes as the tidal level varies.
3 The *backshore zone* lies above the level of wave reach and may comprise previously deposited beach ridges or sand dunes. Only occasionally is the backshore zone affected by waves, during exceptional storms, for example.

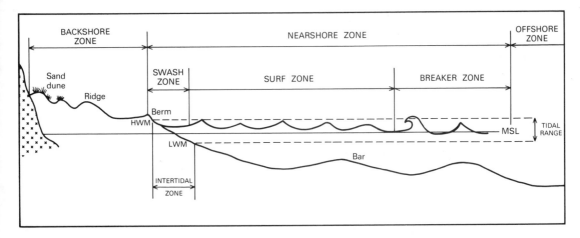

Fig. 1.5 Coastal wave zones and beach features. The swash zone shown relates to high tide and will migrate down the beach as the tide falls.

Within this general framework the various coastal landforms develop. The *beach*, for example, starts where the waves begin to modify themselves in depths of a quarter of the wave length and ends at the limit of wave action. However, a small pocket beach on a rocky coast may be limited to a few metres of the nearshore area, while on a shallow sandy coast it may be several kilometres wide. Beaches (Chapter 4) may be characterised by low accumulations of sediment in the nearshore zone called *bars*. Low *ridges* separated by *runnels* may occur in the intertidal zones of wide sandy beaches with the limit of wave action marked by a flat ridge of sand called a *berm* (Fig. 1.5). Fine sand may be blown by the wind from the intertidal zone into the backshore zone to be deposited in *sand dunes* (Chapter 5). On pebble beaches the *ridge* at the limit of wave action is steeper and more prominent than a sand berm.

On steeper coasts these zones may be considerably narrower and on plunging *cliffs* the waves may not even break (Chapter 3). However, at the foot of most cliffs where the waves remove rock, an overhang or *notch* may develop. As the cliff is eroded backwards, the stump of the eroded cliff remains as a low-gradient or *shore platform*. In sheltered environments many of the coastal landforms are influenced by tidal processes rather than by wave processes. *Mudflats* and their vegetated upper portions or *salt marshes* develop in sheltered environments like *estuaries* (Chapter 6) or in the protection of large-scale coastal depositional features like *spits* and *forelands* (Chapter 4).

In view of the great variety of coastal forms and landscapes, the early preoccupation with classification of coasts is perhaps understandable and this is reviewed below.

Coastal types

There have been many attempts at coastal classification but no completely satisfactory scheme has yet been devised. This is not surprising given the great variation both in coastal forms and in the processes operating on them. Add to this variety the fact that coasts do not adjust to changes in sea-level at the same rate, then the problems of classifying all coasts into one scheme become formidable. A further drawback associated with classifications is that they are primarily concerned with coastal description, whereas the aim of coastal

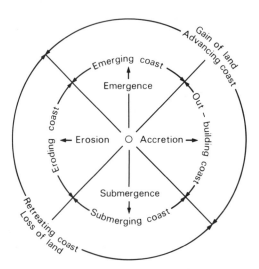

Fig. 1.6 Coastal classification by means of sea-level change. Source: modified from King (1972)

geomorphology is to explain the form in terms of the process. The most successful classifications attempt to incorporate elements of both form *and* process.

The three main groups of classification are based upon variations in (1) sea-level, (2) structure and (3) processes.

Classification based on sea-level variation

The large variation in sea-levels during the Pleistocene period have had a great influence on coastal forms and this has led to the proposal that coasts could be described in terms of submergence and emergence. For example, fjord (Fig. 1.4b) and ria coasts are essentially subaerial valleys flooded by sea-level rise, whereas coastal plains with salt marshes and barrier islands may be emerged segments of flat seabed. However, many coastal types do not conform to these categories and are regarded as neutral. This classification was further developed by subdividing emergent and submergent coasts into those shaped by erosion or deposition. Such a refinement has the merit of recognising that whether a coast advances or retreats is a function not only of sea-level rise and fall but also of sediment deposition and erosion (Fig. 1.6).

Classification based on structural variation

Many coasts and coastal landforms are controlled by variations in geological structure. At the continental scale, coastal evolution can be explained in terms of plate tectonic theory (Fig. 1.7) to identify the following:

1 *Collision coasts* are formed where two plates converge. Such coasts are often straight, being characterised by narrow continental shelves and tectonically unstable mountainous areas inland, e.g. the Andean coast of South America.
2 *Trailing edge coasts* are formed where two plates diverge. Such coasts are fronted by wide continental shelves with large fluvial deltas and have tectonically stable inland areas, e.g. the Carolinas coast of North America.
3 *Marginal sea coasts* are a very diverse group with many of the characteristics of trailing edge coasts and often the sites of fluvial deltas.

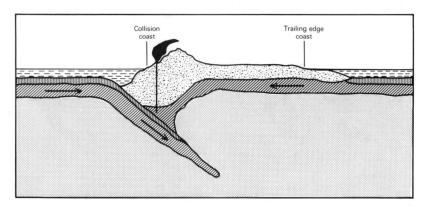

Fig. 1.7 Coastal classification by means of tectonic situation. The cross-section shows a continental plate in collision with an ocean crustal plate creating a collision coast and a trailing edge coast. The crust is the upper part of the rigid rock of the lithosphere. This floats on top of hot fluid rock material known as the asthenosphere. Note the direction of movement of the plates. Source: Davies (1980).

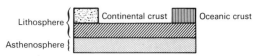

Another structural classification is where the coast is described in terms of its rocks and their resistance to erosion. Bold and low coasts distinguish between bedrock-dominated coast and sedimentary coastal plains. Equally the classification of hard and soft coasts might be used to discriminate between coasts dominated by resistant rocks, cliffs and shore platforms and coasts where sediment deposition is the norm.

Classification based on processes

The modification of present shorelines partly depends upon the amount of wave energy which reaches the coast and so it is possible to classify coasts in terms of wave energy. Coasts can be grouped as follows:

1 *Storm wave environments* where short, high waves from all directions are common, where depositional landforms are at a minimum, and where cliffs and shore platforms are frequent. Such wave environments are found mainly in the storm belts of middle to high latitudes (Fig. 1.8).
2 *Swell wave environments* where waves generated in the storm belts move into lower latitudes and become long, low and consistent in direction. Depositional sandy landforms are common along these coasts.
3 *Protected sea environments* where wave activity is limited by ice cover in high latitudes or where seas are enclosed by land.

Another scheme recognises primary and secondary coasts. Primary coasts have been formed by terrestrial processes and have remained unchanged since the last sea-level rise, while secondary coasts have been substantially modified by marine processes.

Summary

Each of the above classifications has its uses in particular situations yet all are inadequate in some respect. Sea-level-based classifications tend to ignore the complex sea-level histories of parts of the coast and this makes identification difficult. Structural classifications, which are useful at the scale of plate tectonics, become less meaningful at smaller scales and ignore the influence of marine processes. The dynamic classifications of wave environments are useful in identifying the wave

13

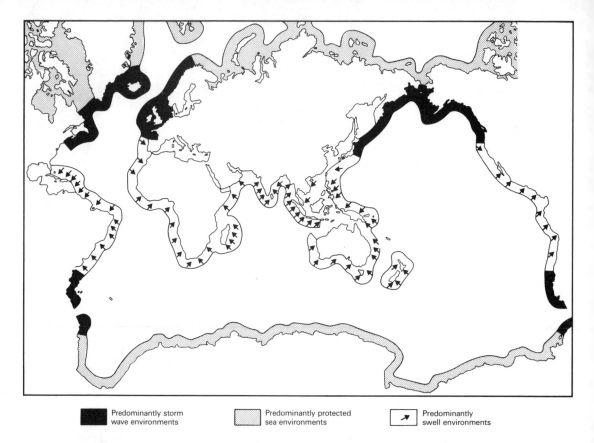

| ■ | Predominantly storm wave environments | ▢ | Predominantly protected sea environments | ↗ | Predominantly swell environments |

Fig. 1.8 Coastal classification by means of wave processes. Low-latitude coasts are mainly influenced by swell waves, mid-latitude coasts by storm waves and high-latitude coasts by protection from waves by ice. Source: adapted from Davies (1980).

processes that affect the coast but say little of coastal outline and landform except where beaches predominate.

Ultimately, classifications do little more than describe the coast, whereas explanation of why the coast varies from place to place rests on an understanding of the processes operating on, and interacting with, the coastal landform. It is the factors that influence these processes that must now be examined.

2 Factors affecting coasts

Coastal landforms develop under the influence of three groups of factors, although the importance of each group varies greatly between coasts. Terrestrial factors relate both to the geological structure of the coast and its influence on landforms, and to the subaerial climatic regime which influences past and present rates of sediment supply to the coast. Marine factors relate to tides, waves and currents, the important sources of energy that modify the coast. Biological factors relate to the effect of plant and animal activity on coastal development.

Terrestrial factors

Structural base

Geological structure can be viewed simply as the container within which all coastal features develop. However, the degree to which structure influences landforms also depends upon the supply of sediment to the coast, and the continuum of coastal types from hard to soft also reflects a transition from structurally dominated coasts to sediment-dominated coasts. The control of structure is best seen along hard, rocky coasts. For example, large-scale folding in the geological past gives rise to distinctive coastal outlines such as the drowned valley landscape of the coast of south-west Ireland (Fig. 2.1a). Geological faults and structural lineation often give rise to very straight coastlines characterised by plunging cliffs or, where they have been exploited by erosional agencies such as glaciers, to fjord coastlines with extensive networks of eroded faults which are now flooded, for example the west coasts of Scotland and Norway (see Fig. 1.4b). At a smaller scale, variations in lithology and structure give rise to promontories where resistant rock occurs and embayments where weaker rocks outcrop (Fig. 2.1b).

Bedrock characteristics are less important on soft coasts since the rock basins are masked to varying degrees by superficial sediments. These sediments are highly mobile and accumulate where wave action is low or moderate or where the supply of sediment far exceeds its removal. Under such conditions bays and inlets become choked with sediment and the bedrock structure is obscured. At a global scale many low-latitude coasts possess a wide fringe of sediment which serves to mask the influence of rock structure. The buffer of sediment between bedrock and shore is noticeably absent from high-latitude coasts and here the influence of structure is much more in evidence. The reasons for such latitudinal disparity in sediment on the coast lie with differences in both the subaerial and marine factors discussed below.

Subaerial processes

While the present climate affects the rate of weathering on coastal cliffs or the build-up of coastal sand dunes, its principal effect on coastal

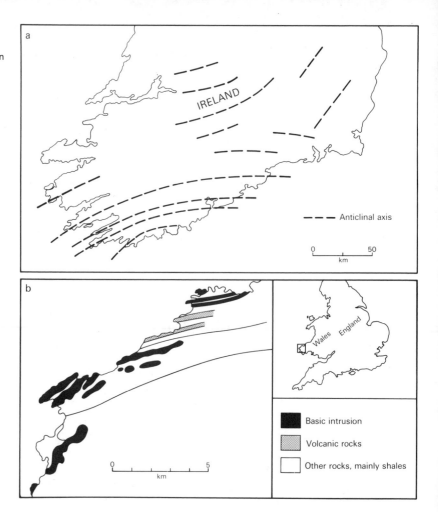

Fig. 2.1(a) Geological folding in the south-west of Ireland has produced a striking series of anticlines which form ridges separated by synclinal valleys which are now flooded by sea-level rise.

(b) The close coincidence between the occurrence of harder igneous rocks and the development of headlands in south-west Wales. Source: modified from Steers (1946).

development lies in the nature and rate of supply of terrestrial sediment to the coast. Climate is an important control on the rainfall, vegetation type and fluvial discharge and consequently it affects denudation of the coastal hinterland. As a general rule, rivers in the tropical-wet and semi-arid zones deliver the maximum amounts of sediment to coasts. Input of sand to the coast is greatest in arid and semi-arid regions where the rivers carry relatively high sediment loads. The Colorado River in the USA and the Orange River in South Africa rank 52nd and 54th respectively in terms of discharge, but 12th and 13th in terms of sediment load. Hot wet coasts tend to be characterised by large inputs of muddy sediments which often form the basis for mangrove swamp development. In higher latitudes large quantities of pebbles occur on the coast, possibly as a result of the relative importance of wave quarrying but also as a result of past and present glacial and fluvio-glacial action (Fig. 2.2).

Superimposed upon these global trends are variations caused by the local influence of sediments either from a river mouth or from the erosion of such soft cliff deposits as glacial tills. One striking variation is the sediment input into trailing edge or marginal sea coasts (see p. 12) by rivers which flow from tectonically active coasts on the far side of the continental plate. Both of these coastal types are the sites of most of the world's major river mouths and deltas, e.g. the Amazon delta in Brazil

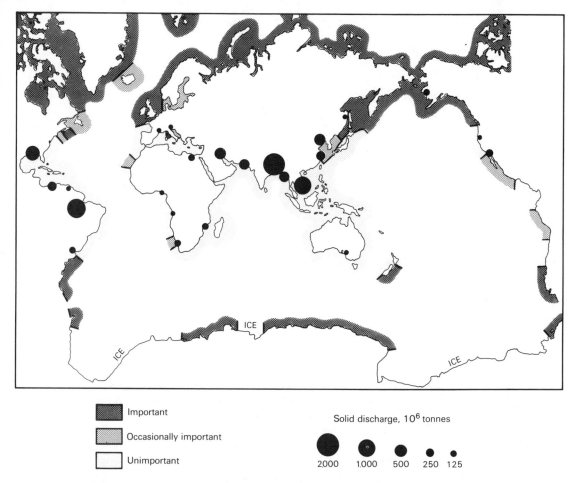

Important

Occasionally important

Unimportant

Solid discharge, 10^6 tonnes

2000   1,000   500   250   125

Fig. 2.2 The relative global importance of pebbles as beach materials and the amount of sediment discharged by the major rivers of the world. Source: adapted from Davies (1980).

(Fig. 2.2). Even so there is a clear low-latitude bias in the location of large inputs of fluvial sediments.

Fluvial sediment of about 0.063 mm and coarser may remain as beach material; the rest is lost offshore. However, in areas where rivers enter the coast via estuaries or inlets, deposition inside the inlet may prevent the sediment actually reaching the outer coast. Ultimately such inlets are filled with sediment and direct contributions to the outer coast can begin, but this takes time. As discussed later, this has important implications for tackling the problem of coastal erosion. The eventual form of the coast depends not only on structure and sediment availability but also on the extent of modification by both marine and biological agents. These factors are examined next.

Marine factors

Tides

It has long been recognised that tides affect coastal development, yet their precise role is less clear. These regular and predictable rises and falls of sea-level are important because they increase the vertical range across which wave activity can take place. Tides are also responsible for currents which move sediments, particularly near to coastal constrictions like bay or harbour entrances.

Tides are caused by the gravitational pull of the moon and – to a

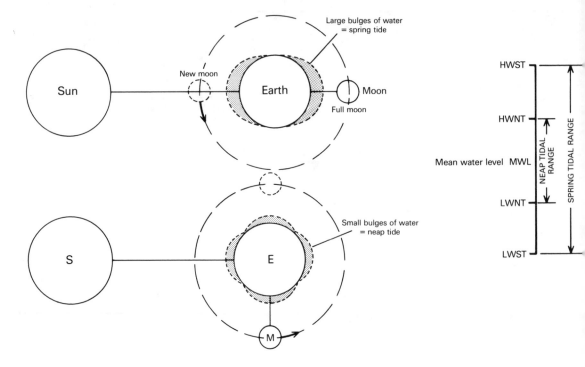

Fig. 2.3 The generation of tides. Spring tides or maximum tidal range are produced when sun, moon and earth are in alignment whereas neap tides or minimum tidal range are produced when sun and moon act in opposition to one another.

lesser extent – the sun, on the earth. As water is less viscous than other earth materials, it responds by bulging up in the direction of pull. However, there is also a bulge produced by the so-called centrifugal force on the opposite side of the earth, i.e. facing away from the moon. Since the earth is rotating the bulges appear to travel round the surface creating two tides per day at most locations. (These true tidal waves should not be confused with tsunamis or shock waves which are produced by earthquake or volcanic eruption.) The strongest or spring tides occur twice-monthly when the sun, earth and moon are in alignment so that the gravitational force of the sun is added to that of the moon (Fig. 2.3). The weakest or neap tides occur when the sun, earth and moon are at 90° to each other so that sun and moon act in opposition.

This simple pattern gives rise to regular tidal variations in time. However, tidal variation from place to place is influenced by the blocking effect of landmasses and the geometry of the ocean basins. The advancing tidal wave is reflected in varying degrees by coastal outlines, leading to different tidal ranges around coasts. In addition, as the tide is in fact a wave of very long wave length it becomes greatly modified in shallow water. The irregular outline and shallow depth of the North Sea, for example (Fig. 2.4), results in the coasts of Norway and Denmark having limited tidal ranges and the north-east coast of Britain a large tidal range. One of the most dramatic differences can be seen by comparing the 2m range of the English south coast with the 8m tidal range of the Normandy coast just across the English Channel. Where the tidal wave enters a bay or estuary, exceptionally high tides can result. As the tidal wave moves into the narrowing embayment, the water is funnelled and this raises the height. Further, if the embayment is long then the reflected tidal wave may not reach the mouth before the next wave reaches it 12½ hours later. The resultant constructive interference greatly increases the tidal range within the bay. The Bay of

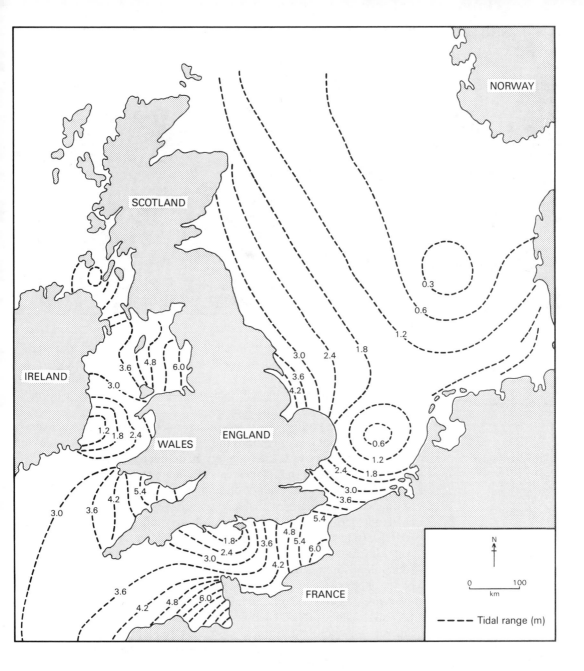

Fig. 2.4 Tidal ranges around Britain. The circular areas of minimum tidal range are known as amphidromic points and are areas around which the advancing tidal wave rotates (anticlockwise in the northern hemisphere owing to deflection to the right by the Coriolis force). Away from these areas tidal ranges are greater. Source: modified from King (1972).

Fundy in Canada has 15.6 m tides at its head and just 3 m tides at the entrance!

These contrasts in tidal range may have repercussions on coastal morphology. For example, a small tidal range limits the vertical extent of any wave action and so it becomes concentrated to produce narrow beaches of limited height. A concentration of wave energy on a limited vertical range may also serve to increase cliff erosion. It follows that where tidal range is limited, wave-produced forms are more common, and where tidal range is great, the influence of tides on morphology is enhanced: Pethick (1984) suggests that the occurrence of wave-dominated forms like spits along the British coast coincides with tidal ranges of 3 m or less. Broad intertidal zones occur where tidal range is great, for example 20 km of tidal flats are exposed in the Bay of

19

Fig. 2.5 Mudflat and salt marsh development in a sheltered estuarine site at Walney Island, Cumbria. Sites like this, with a large tidal range, are conducive to mudflat development.

St Michel in northern France. In sheltered locations with a large tidal range, tidal landforms such as mudflats and salt marshes develop to their maximum extent (Fig. 2.5). Large tidal ranges also produce strong currents capable of moving substantial amounts of sediment, especially through narrow bay entrances.

Meteorological effects on tides can have devastating consequences. During atmospheric depressions the sea surface is forced to rise into the pressure deficiency by 0.1 m for every 10 millibar pressure-fall. Elevations above normal tidal levels of 1 m are thus fairly common in European waters as a result of these *storm surges*. In addition, the strong winds associated with depressions have an effect: offshore winds tend to lower water levels whereas onshore winds pile water against the coast, raising the level. In 1953 a northerly gale in the North Sea raised water levels in east England by 3 m, causing widespread flooding up to 6 km inland and resulting in the deaths of 307 people. In the Netherlands the same storm led to the deaths of 1,800 people and to the evacuation of 100,000 others. In 1970 a storm surge in the Bay of Bengal drowned 700,000 people and altered the coastline of the Sundarbans overnight. Television screens frequently display the effects of the 6 m hurricane-induced storm surges experienced on the Gulf of Mexico coast of the USA.

Waves in deep water

The principal source of energy input into the coastal zone comes from wind-generated waves. The turbulent effect of wind at sea creates waves which grow owing to pressure differences between the windward and leeward faces. The complex and irregular surface so produced is composed of waves of several sizes travelling in various directions. Fortunately, these combinations of waves can be analysed and described in terms of the following:

> amplitude or height from crest to trough (H),
> frequency or period between successive crests (T),
> wave length or distance from crest to crest (L) (Fig. 2.6).

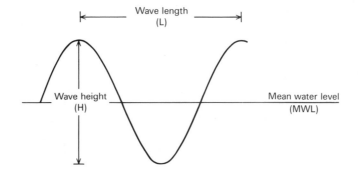

Fig. 2.6 Definition of basic wave parameters.

Thus wave steepness or slope is given by the ratio H_o/L_o, and wave velocity (C) by the formula

$$C_o = \frac{L_o}{T} \quad \text{where} \quad _o \text{ denotes deep water.}$$

In water deeper than $L_o/4$, the relationship between wave length and wave period is expressed thus:

1 $L_o = 1.56\,T^2$ so that
2 $C_o = 1.56\,T$

Since the energy of a wave, E (per unit width of wave crest), is related to the square of the wave height,

3 $E = \frac{1}{8}\,\rho g H^2 \quad \text{where} \quad \begin{aligned}&\rho = \text{water density}\\ &g = \text{acceleration due to gravity}\end{aligned}$

then any wave can be accurately described and its energy assessed by measuring wave height and period. The movement of this energy over the surface is known as wave power (P) and is governed by the wave velocity (C):

4 $P = ECn \quad \text{where} \quad \begin{aligned}&Cn = \text{velocity of the wave group; in shallow}\\ &\text{water n} = 1.\end{aligned}$

Equations (1) and (2) are important since they indicate that small increases in wave period are associated with large increases in wave length, and that longer waves move faster than short ones. Longer waves emerge from the area of a storm in advance of shorter waves and therefore sort themselves into groups of similar velocities. By the time that these long, flat *swell waves* have reached a distant shore they have become very regular indeed. Conversely, within the storm generation area both long and short waves are produced at the same time, giving a complex irregular appearance to these storm or *sea waves*. The importance of equation (3) lies in the relationship of wave energy with wave height: small increases in wave height lead to large increases in wave energy. In stormy areas where the generation of high and steep waves might be expected, much of the wave energy actually reaches the coast to perform geomorphological work.

Since the storm belts of the world are mainly confined to latitudes of 30° or more, it is possible to identify global storm wave, swell wave and protected sea environments (see Fig. 1.8). It follows that coasts predominantly subject to the regularity of long, flat swell waves will develop different coastal forms from those subject to the irregularity of high, steep storm waves.

21

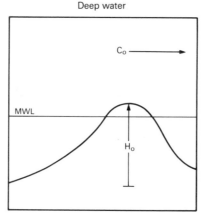

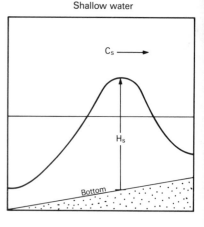

Fig. 2.7 The increase in wave height (potential energy) is accommodated by a decrease in wave velocity (kinetic energy) as the wave shoals in shallowing water. Subscript 'o' refers to deep water waves and subscript 's' to shallow water waves.

Deep water

Shallow water

Waves in shallow water

Transformation of waves entering shallow water begins as the wave 'touches bottom' at depths of approximately $L_o/2$ (also known as the wave base), but significant changes occur at depths of approximately $L_o/20$. If waves are regarded as simple energy systems, wave energy is conserved into shallow water since losses due to bottom drag are minimal. Transformation is due to a redistribution of energy within the wave itself. However, in shallow water wave velocity is affected by water depth in the following way:

5 $\quad C_s = gd \quad$ where $\quad d =$ water depth

so that as the water becomes shallower, wave velocity decreases. If conservation of energy is to be upheld then wave energy must be redistributed to compensate for a reduction in speed. As energy is directly related to the square of wave height then this transformation is manifest in the familiar increase in wave height in shallowing water (Fig. 2.7).

The fall in wave velocity as water depth decreases has another major effect on wave behaviour. Most waves approach the coastline at an oblique angle, so one section of the wave crest is in shallow water while the seaward section is in deeper water. Since velocity is related to water depth (equation (5)) the shallow-water section of the wave will move more slowly than the section in deeper water and cause the wave crest to bend until all parts of the crest are in water of equal depth (Fig. 2.8). This is the process of *wave refraction* and it results in either the spreading out (divergence) or the focusing (convergence) of wave energy. The effect of refraction on wave energy is best described by considering *wave rays* or lines drawn at right-angles to the wave crests. Between each pair of adjacent wave rays, the wave power (ρ) is assumed to be constant so that wave energy and thus wave height increases where rays converge and decreases where they diverge.

When waves enter shallowing water, the wave height increases rapidly along with the wave steepness. Steepness increases up to a point where the wave becomes unstable and breaks. Waves break because the velocity of water particles in the crest exceeds the velocity of the wave itself, leading to water breaking through the wave form. There are three types of breaker: spilling, plunging and surging. Spilling breakers are associated with steep waves and flat beaches; spilling begins some distance from the shore, the slight foaming of each wave crest becoming

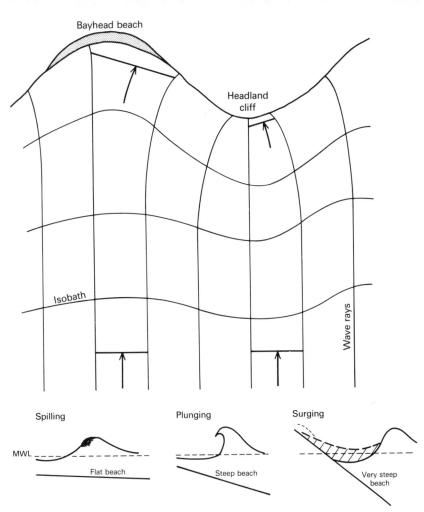

Fig. 2.8 The refraction (bending) of wave crests as they approach the coast. Since wave energy is thought to be conserved *within* adjacent wave rays, refraction of the waves spreads the available energy over a wider area in bays and focuses the energy over a narrower area at headlands.

Bayhead beach

Headland cliff

Isobath

Wave rays

Fig. 2.9 Types of breaking wave and the beaches on which they commonly occur. Source: Clark (1979).

Spilling

Plunging

Surging

MWL

Flat beach

Steep beach

Very steep beach

wider and producing a band of surf as it moves shorewards (Fig. 2.9). Plunging breakers occur on steep beaches when the leading edge of a wave becomes almost vertical, the top curling over and plunging forwards. Surging breakers occur close to very steep beaches that are subject to waves of low steepness. These peak as if to break but the base of the wave hits the beach and surges up, leaving the crest to collapse.

Wave-induced currents

There are two types of wave-induced current: shore-normal currents and shore-parallel or longshore currents. These currents are responsible for the movement of most coastal sediment and for changes in coastal morphology.

1 *Shore-normal currents* are produced by the orbital motion of water particles in waves as water depths decrease (Fig. 2.10). In depths of $L_o/20$ or less, the orbits become ellipses which ultimately flatten so much that water moves onshore and offshore along a line. However, the onshore and offshore velocities of these reversing currents are not equal: the onshore velocity increases in magnitude but declines in duration. Ultimately this asymmetry is manifest in a high-velocity but short-duration swash or water uprush on the beach, followed by a low-velocity but long-duration backwash of water down the beach.

Fig. 2.10 As the wave moves towards shallower water, the circular orbits of the water particles become increasingly elliptical until they eventually move back and forth along a line.

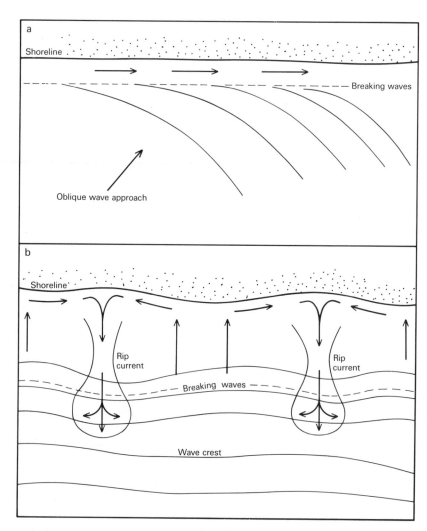

Fig. 2.11 Longshore currents due to (a) oblique wave approach and (b) cell circulation systems.

These currents are responsible for the movement of sediment on and offshore.

2 *Longshore currents* are generated by differences in wave height along the beach or by an oblique wave approach. Following refraction it is common to find some residual obliqueness in waves and this imparts a longshore component (P_l) to the energy directed towards the shore:

$$P_l = ECn \sin \alpha \cos \alpha \qquad \text{where} \quad \begin{aligned} P_l &= \text{longshore power} \\ \alpha &= \text{angle of wave approach} \end{aligned}$$

This longshore current acts parallel to the coastline and is responsible

Fig. 2.12 Beach cusps and other related forms may be the result of small-scale cell circulation systems created by interference patterns between incident and trapped 'edge' waves. Morecambe Bay, Lancashire.

for the movement of large quantities of beach material (Fig. 2.11a).

These two types of wave-induced current appear self-contained and distinct yet on many beaches they co-exist and overlap in *cell circulation systems*. These cell systems consist of onshore and longshore currents feeding strong, narrow and dangerous rip currents which flow seawards through the breaker zone (Fig. 2.11b). Because rip currents are narrow, swimmers caught by them should attempt to swim alongshore rather than exhaust themselves swimming against the current. Water levels shorewards of areas of high waves are greater than those opposite low-wave areas. There is a head of water between these beach areas, and a longshore current moves in both directions away from the area of high water levels. The two opposing longshore currents meet and flow seawards as a rip current at the position of lowest wave heights.

Some cell systems may be generated by wave height differences caused by refraction over an uneven seabed, yet regularly spaced cell systems exist on long straight beaches with a uniform seabed. The most plausible explanation for regularly spaced areas of high and low waves is that the incoming waves generate a secondary set of waves that are trapped within the surf zone. These *edge waves*, as they are called, interact with the incoming waves to create a regular system of high and low waves. The significance of such circulation lies in the understanding of rhythmic coastal topography such as beach cusps (Fig. 2.12). The influence of wave-induced currents on the development of coastal landforms cannot be overestimated since they are the principal way in which sediment is moved on and offshore and alongshore.

Biological factors

Vegetation

Virtually all newly created land surfaces are potential sites of plant colonisation and in the coastal environment pioneer species readily invade the more stable parts of recently deposited features. A two-way relationship exists between coastal plants and landforms because the presence of plants often enhances the depositional processes that created the landform itself. The plants which initially colonise *beaches* and *sand dunes* do so in areas that are infrequently disturbed by inundation at the rear of the beach. Salt-tolerant species are the first colonisers of sandy beaches and as the frequency of tidal inundation decreases up the beach, species such as marram grass (*Ammophila arenaria*) become more common. These plants are very successful because of their capacity to produce horizontal and vertical shoots or rhizomes which extend from the parent plant. This characteristic ensures the effective colonisation of new sand surfaces and a rapid response to burial of the plant by sand. *Salt-marsh* vegetation performs a similar function since it promotes deposition in mudflat environments. Salt marshes are colonised by salt-tolerant plants like marsh samphire (*Salicornia* spp.). As a result of this colonisation, the deposition of sediment increases, the marsh grows in height and the frequency of tidal inundation decreases.

In the hot and wet tropics, *mangrove* trees dominate areas that would otherwise support salt-marsh vegetation. Mangrove trees produce numerous roots which radiate away from the parent tree (Fig. 2.13). These extensive root systems help to bind the mud together and enhance deposition. In spite of the clear vegetational contrasts between

Fig. 2.13 Tidal mangrove swamp at Nusa Dua, Bali, Indonesia. The tropical equivalent of a salt marsh, mangroves have prop roots (visible in the foreground) which help bind the tidal mud together. Photo: Elizabeth Clutton.

salt marsh and mangrove, the landform that is colonised and the ensuing enhanced deposition show remarkable similarities across the latitudes.

Some species of *marine algae* produce nodules or films of carbonate material which can accumulate as a cemented mass in calcareous banks and reefs offshore, and as individual calcareous fragments in beach material. *Lithothamnion* is the most common of these species in both tropical and higher latitudes. The so-called coral beaches of the Isle of Skye, Scotland, are mainly composed of such fragments. In contrast, the blue-green algae erode rock by secreting oxalic acid which dissolves calcium carbonate, often to a depth of several millimetres.

Animals

Several species of marine animals exploit coastal rocks for food and shelter. Intertidal and subtidal molluscs browse on the algae that inhabit rock surfaces and remove rock in the process. Other molluscs bore into coastal rock both weakening it and making it more susceptible to erosion. The wrinkled rock borer (*Hiatella arctica*) successfully bores into hard limestones for protection, the piddock (*Pholas dactylus*) bores into softer chalk, sandstones and shales, and the usually free-living algal browsing sea urchin (*Paracentrotus lividus*) bores into the limestones and shales of Co. Clare, Ireland, for shelter where wave exposure is great.

Apart from the calcareous algae, the most important constructive marine organisms are the *coral* species. The landforms created by the coral polyps are impressive: the Great Barrier Reefs off the eastern coast of Australia extend for about 1,750 km. The distribution of coral reefs and of the polyps which build them is controlled mainly by temperature, the limits lying close to the sea surface isotherm of 20°C for the coldest month. The polyps take up calcium carbonate in the sea water and grow into various skeletal structures. Calcareous algae and molluscs which co-habit with the corals fill in the skeletal structures to form the calcareous mass of a reef limestone. The features are known as fringing reefs where they adjoin the coast, barrier reefs where they lie offshore and atolls where they encircle an offshore lagoon. Not only do coral reefs represent one of the most potent forms of organic deposition on the coast but their presence offshore substantially reduces the wave and current processes operating on the shore.

3 Erosional processes and forms

Fig. 3.1 Vertical cliffs and arches are cut in horizontally bedded shales near Loop Head in Co. Clare, Ireland. Collapse of the arch by wave undermining will eventually result in the formation of a stack.

Plunging sea cliffs and extensive shore platforms are the most commonly described forms of coastal erosion (Fig. 3.1). However, the shape of many coastal cliffs owes as much to past and present subaerial action as to marine processes. For example, the final coastal form may be a glacial trough wall which has been flooded by marine inundation or a smooth, rounded solifluction slope steepened by marine undercutting. All slope forms are controlled by the rate at which weathered debris accumulates at the slope foot. Coastal cliffs are no exception to this general rule of slope form. On most cliff coasts the amount of debris produced by mass-movement is less than the amount removed by waves and currents and so slopes tend to be steep, especially where the cliffs are exposed to high-energy storm waves which undercut the cliff face and rapidly remove the collapsed debris (Fig. 3.2). Any reduction in the amount of debris removed by waves, or increase in the rate of debris supplied by subaerial processes, may lead to the development of a small beach and eventually to a talus slope masking the foot of the cliff. Where subaerial processes supply debris at a far greater rate than the rate of removal by wave processes, lower-angled cliffs result. For example, at Barton-on-Sea in Hampshire, the sheer volume of sediment from coastal landslides prevents waves from removing sufficient sediment to form steep cliffs (Fig. 3.3). Coastal slopes are subaerial slopes that have been trimmed at their base by marine processes. These processes must also operate on the shore platform at the foot of the cliffs since this feature represents the eroded remnant of the original coastal slope. It is therefore possible to examine the marine processes

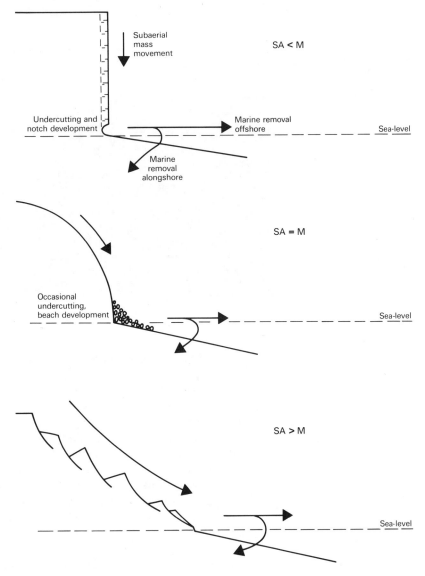

Fig. 3.2 Processes of cliff retreat. Where marine (M) processes exceed subaerial (SA) delivery of sediment or rocks, the cliff is undermined and retreats. Where subaerial processes dominate, a low-angled slope results. Where marine undercutting is less frequent owing to a balance between marine and subaerial processes, a beach may develop. Source: modified from Davies (1980).

together to investigate how they influence both cliff and shore platform morphology.

Marine processes of erosion

Four main groups of marine erosion process can be identified: mechanical wave erosion, weathering, solution and bio-erosion.

Mechanical wave erosion

This comprises two distinct processes, wave quarrying and abrasion.

1 *Wave quarrying* is identified by the prising or pulling away of pieces of rock by the shock of impact of breaking waves. Secondary processes may also be involved, for example pressure release as rock is eroded and the pneumatic effects of air pressure in rock crevices. Recent research has suggested that pressure variations caused by the orbital motion of waves weakens rocks in situ, although these effects

Fig. 3.3 Failure of clay and earth cliffs during wet stormy weather results in a low-angled but unstable cliff that is prone to continued erosion. Barton-on-Sea, Hampshire.

are only likely to be significant in soft rock, such as glacial till, and on shore platforms which the waves traverse. The structure of the rock is important since those rocks which have a well-developed cleavage and jointing and those which are soft and unconsolidated will be more prone to quarrying. Fresh rock scars and loose fragments on cliffs and shore platforms have been used as examples of the efficiency of wave quarrying but only recently has experimental information begun to appear. Experiments on model cliffs in a wave tank show that the pressure exerted by breaking waves causes the greatest amount of quarrying; broken waves are the next most effective; and unbroken waves reflected by the cliff in deep water cause negligible erosion (Fig. 3.4). Maximum quarrying is found on cliffs fronted by narrow, steep beaches which induce wave-breaking. The erosion of cliffs is further enhanced by the availability of abrasive materials, such as pebbles and small boulders, that are moved by the waves against the cliff foot or across the shore platform (Fig. 3.5).

2   *Abrasion* is the process by which rocks are mechanically worn down by wave-moved sediment. Quarrying and abrasion work best together and in time they produce notching of the cliff base. The efficiency of abrasion is likely to be enhanced if the abrasives are of a harder rock than the cliff itself, e.g. flint pebbles abrading a chalk cliff.

The production of a shore platform by abrasion and quarrying is a good example of a self-regulating process, since the wave erosion of the cliff foot declines in frequency and efficiency as the shore platform widens. Erosion by quarrying and abrasion then shifts onto the shore platform itself.

Weathering

Cliffs and shore platforms are subject to two types of weathering process: water layer weathering and subaerial weathering.

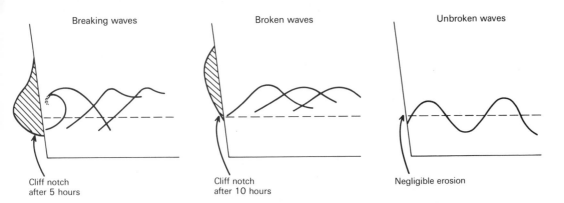

Breaking waves — Cliff notch after 5 hours

Broken waves — Cliff notch after 10 hours

Unbroken waves — Negligible erosion

Fig. 3.4 Wave-tank simulation of the erosion of a vertical cliff under breaking, broken and unbroken wave attack. Source: Sunamura (1975).

Fig. 3.5 Abrasion of the cliff foot and shore platform is most effective where there is a plentiful supply of abrasives. In this example, the boulders comprising the abrasive medium are themselves worn down as well as the rock surface.

1 *Water layer weathering* relates to the tidal wetting and drying of the cliff and platform by waves, spray and tides. Salt crystallisation and swelling within cracks and crevices causes the mechanical breakdown of the rock surfaces in the zone of frequent wetting and drying. Pitting or honeycombing of cliff faces within the spray zone is evidence of these processes and is particularly noticeable in sandstones and other sedimentary rocks where the cementing material becomes decomposed. The process reduces in efficiency as the frequency of wetting and drying decreases both higher up the cliff face and lower down where the rock is permanently saturated.

2 *Subaerial weathering* relates to the processes of normal weathering which loosen rock surfaces and deliver debris to the cliff foot. Wave action subsequently removes the debris. In the coastal areas of mid and high latitudes, where temperatures may fall below freezing, the most potent form of such weathering is the action of frost. Coastal cliff retreat in polar areas owes much to freezing associated with fresh water or snowmelt and, in spite of the lower freezing point of salt water, frost action on the shore platform itself occurs at low tide. Such frost action may well be partly responsible for the wide subhorizontal shore platforms found in polar regions and for some wide shore platforms in Britain which are thought to have been partly eroded during the dying phases of the last glaciation.

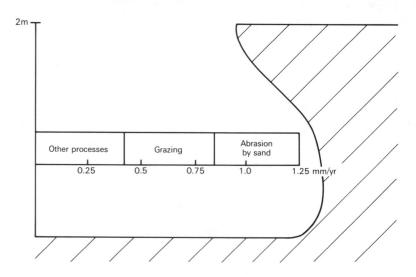

Fig. 3.6 Rates of intertidal notch erosion in limestone, Aldabra Atoll, Indian Ocean. Source: Trudgill (1985).

Solution

Solutional processes are generally thought to be most important in calcareous rock types where sea water heavily charged with dissolved carbon dioxide aggressively dissolves the coastal rock. Such reactions are assisted by the frequent water changes which occur in the surf zone. In theory the concentration of carbon dioxide decreases in warmer waters, so it is surprising that solution appears to be an important process on tropical coasts. It is possible that this chemical disadvantage is more than offset by the combined effects of an abundance of calcareous rocks in the tropics and the enhanced solutional aggression caused by overnight production of carbon dioxide by abundant marine plants in tropical rock pools. It also seems likely that the lower wave energy of tropical coasts reduces the amount of wave erosion to a level where solutional effects become more evident. Since rock pools in calcareous rocks are popular habitats for marine organisms which actively erode rock, solutional processes are often difficult to separate from bio-erosion.

Bio-erosion

Living organisms in all nearshore zones contribute actively to the erosion of rock, but the effects are most marked in the tropics, where biological activity in calcareous rocks appears to reach a maximum. Many molluscs, sea urchins and fish graze rock surfaces in search of algae. Since some algae grow within the rock as well as on the surface, there are several levels of grazing, which leads to the removal of layers of rock by the rasping tongues of grazing organisms. Some sponges, bivalves, barnacles and sea urchins bore into the rock in search of food or shelter. That bio-erosion occurs is beyond question but what is more contentious is the extent to which these organisms produce coastal landforms. In all areas except the tropics, wave erosion greatly outweighs bio-erosion and so the biological effect may be reduced to colonisation of suitable habitats originally produced by wave erosion. On tropical coasts the relationships between organisms and landforms are clearer and several studies relate undercut notches in limestones to bio-erosion (Fig. 3.6).

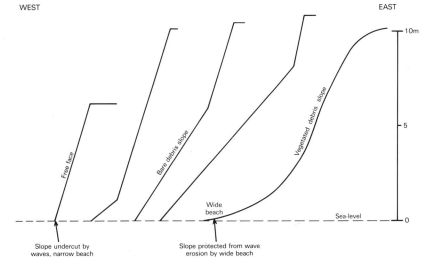

WEST   EAST

Fig. 3.7 The form of these cliffs in the Solent is related to the occurrence of beaches which offer varying degrees of protection to the cliff foot.
Source: Clark and Small (1982).

The form of coastal cliffs

Variation in the morphology of coastal cliffs may be caused by the degree of exposure to wave attack; the most spectacular cliffs are associated with maximum wave activity (see Fig. 3.1) and degraded cliffs with less wave activity. There are numerous examples of coasts where part of the cliff line is subject to vigorous wave action yet adjacent parts of the same cliff are protected either by a sheltering headland or by beach development (Fig. 3.7). Other factors which contribute to cliff form are the geomorphology of the hinterland, the lithology and structure of the rock, and the history of sea-level change.

Other things being equal, cliffs formed in higher ground at the coast erode more slowly than cliffs formed in lower ground and so they tend to form headlands. Since the interfluves and higher ground are frequently underlain by more resistant rocks, high cliffs also tend to be associated with more resistant rocks. Impermeable crystalline rocks are highly resistant to wave erosion whereas sedimentary rocks are more susceptible, especially where the solution of the rock cement aids disintegration. Some lithologies produce characteristic forms. Clay formations undergo slumping during wet weather leading to a low-angled profile composed of several rotational slip units, e.g. Christchurch Bay in Hampshire. Massive chalk formations produce near-vertical cliffs on both sides of the English Channel and basalts give rise to distinctive stepped cliff profiles in the Isle of Skye, Scotland, and in Iceland and the Faeroes. A good example of the importance of lithology is seen on the west coast of Wales where the intricacies of headland and bay are directly related to the occurrence of harder igneous rocks (see Fig. 2.1b).

Rock structure also plays an important role because, irrespective of lithology, massive and uniform rocks erode less slowly than rocks shattered by faulting or with closely spaced joints and bedding surfaces. Well-jointed and bedded sedimentary rocks like sandstones are exploited by weathering and wave erosion to produce the arches, stacks, geos and blowholes that are common on our coasts (Fig. 3.1). Horizontally bedded rocks favour the development of steep cliffs, arches and stacks because the removal of higher blocks depends on the

33

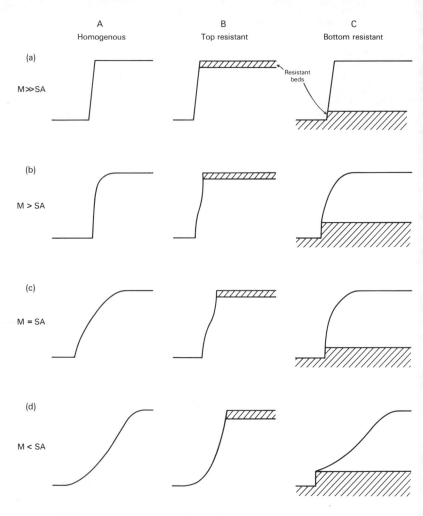

Fig. 3.8 A classification of active sea-cliff forms produced in three types of rock configuration by four combinations of marine (M) and subaerial (SA) process regimes. Source: Emery and Kuhn (1982).

prior removal of lower blocks, initially by notch development at wave level (Fig. 1.4a). Vertical or near-vertical beds produce lower cliff angles that are more related to the rate of subaerial weathering of the cliff top than marine erosion of the cliff foot. Seaward-dipping beds that are undercut by wave activity are characterised by slab-failure along the bedding planes; the bare coastal slope then assumes the angle of dip as in the shale cliffs at Morfa Buchan in Dyfed.

Because of the many combinations of process, lithology and structure, generalisation of cliff form is hazardous. Nevertheless, classification of active sea-cliff profiles based on the interaction of process and geology is possible (Fig. 3.8). Such approaches take little account of the infinite variations in structure and hinterland geomorphology. Clearly, cliffs erode into a variety of pre-existing topographic situations (e.g. river valleys and interfluves trending at all angles to the coast) and into a variety of structures (e.g. alternating layers of resistant and less resistant rock bands). In addition, many cliffs owe much to changes of sea-level and climate in the geologically recent past. Plunging cliffs, for example, are widely thought to be unmodified by processes at present sea-level since most of the wave energy is reflected and little erosion takes place. Many cliffs and shore platforms are demonstrably older than the last glaciation since they are draped with glacial till that has been only partly removed by present wave activity. These ancient cliffs and platforms often trend at an angle to the present coast, as at Sewerby near Flamborough Head in Humberside.

Cliffs often exhibit two distinct profiles: an upper slope or bevel and a steep, lower free face. These 'slope-over-walls' are thought to reflect intense periglacial weathering of the original cliff during the Pleistocene cold period when sea-levels were low. Subsequent removal of the loose debris occurred when sea-level rose to its present position. The lower parts of the debris slope were trimmed back to bedrock leaving the upper slope intact. The cliffs of Start Bay in Devon are good examples of this.

The form of shore platforms

The most useful generalisation of shore platform morphology recognises intertidal, high tide and low tide platforms that are directly related to the major groups of processes already discussed (Fig. 3.9). However, as with generalisation about cliff form, these model shore platforms must be seen as ideal forms which will vary depending on site-specific circumstances such as rock type and sea-level history.

Fig. 3.9 The major shore platform types. Source: Bird (1984).

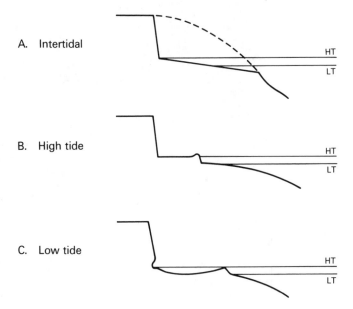

Intertidal platforms

These are produced by quarrying and abrasion and are best formed in areas of high wave energy and easily quarried rock. Since the height of the inner edge of the platform is related to wave height and the outer edge to the depth limit of quarrying and abrasion, such mechanically eroded platforms display a slope or ramp from high tide to low tide level. The slope, however, is rarely regular since variations in rock type and structure are exploited by wave erosion to produce an irregular surface. Sloping intertidal platforms are very common in the storm wave environments of the mid latitudes. Well-developed intertidal platforms occur in south Wales and on the north Yorkshire coast at

35

Fig. 3.10(a) A sloping intertidal shore platform at Quilty, Co. Clare, Ireland. Abrasion and quarrying are important processes and the platform surface may be littered with rock fragments.

(b) A high tide shore platform near Marseilles on the moderate to low wave energy French Mediterranean coast. The surface is washed at high tide leading to water layer weathering and active notch development.

(c) A well-developed low tide shore platform eroded in Pleistocene dune limestones on the Nepean coast of Victoria, Australia where solutional processes are important.

a

b

c

Whitby. The degree of slope is related to the tidal range: steep slopes are found where wave energy is spread vertically by a large tidal range and low gradients occur where tidal range is restricted (Fig. 3.10a).

High tide platforms

These platforms are produced by the alternate wetting and drying of rocks. Because such processes operate up to the limit of saturation, these platforms develop close to the high water mark and generally have a near-horizontal surface terminated abruptly by a cliff to low water mark. At the seaward edge there may be a ridge formed by the slower rate of water layer weathering in the zone where spray keeps the rocks constantly wet. High tide platforms tend to form best where rocks are permeable and horizontally bedded, where evaporation rates are high and where tidal characteristics allow a long drying period. Since quarrying and abrasion processes rapidly destroy the features produced by slower weathering, high tide platforms are preserved best where mechanical wave erosion is limited. On all counts, low latitude coasts are the most favoured for such platform development. Good examples occur on the high evaporation and microtidal coasts of the Mediterranean (Fig. 3.10b).

Low tide platforms

Platforms of this type are produced by solution and biological erosion and since these processes operate down to low water mark, this is the minimum altitude at which such platforms develop. However, some lie well above this level depending on the environmental tolerance of the species involved. A further complication lies in the difficulty in discriminating between platforms produced by bio-erosion and those constructed by organisms such as corals and calcareous algae which may build above low water mark. Low tide platforms generally develop by solution and bio-erosion in the notch at the rear of the platform. Common in tropical areas, they are also found on mid latitude limestone coasts where bio-erosion and solution occur, e.g. on the limestone coast of Victoria, Australia (Fig. 3.10c).

4 Depositional processes and forms

The same waves that cause erosion and retreat of rock coasts also move sediment within the coastal zone. Finer sediments are moved by wave or tidal currents to settle in sheltered areas or far offshore where waves rarely disturb the sea floor. Within the zone where waves affect the bottom, sand and pebble calibres tend to be concentrated into beaches at the limit of wave activity. Larger pebbles and boulders are only moved in exceptionally stormy conditions. Before examining depositional processes and forms, it is useful to outline the nature, sources and losses of sediment in the coastal system.

Coastal sediment

Characteristics of coastal sediment

The study of coastal sediments is important because of the information that can be derived from them about coastal processes. For example, beaches composed of large, well-rounded pebbles are likely to exist in high wave energy environments; the movement of such coarse particles is confined to storm wave activity. The most important characteristics of coastal sediment are particle size and sorting.

The main sediment types found in coastal environments are muds, sands and pebbles. The mean grain size is a good indicator of the water velocity required to move that calibre of sediment. Moderate velocities of about 0.2 ms^{-1} will move most sand grains but higher velocities are required to move both coarser pebbles and the more cohesive sediments like muds. Sorting is directly related to the degree to which waves or wind can segregate sediment according to size: good sorting indicates selective action in transporting a limited range of calibres; poor sorting shows little selection resulting in a sediment with a mixture of calibres.

On a world scale there are variations in the importance of muds, sands and pebbles. The importance of pebbles as beach materials in the higher latitudes is linked to the greater quarrying ability of waves and to the availability of coarse sediments derived from Pleistocene glacial deposits (see Fig. 2.2). Hot wet tropical coasts, on the other hand, are dominated by mud deposits. Sand is found in large quantities everywhere but it assumes particular importance in the arid, semi-arid and rainy areas. Such global variations emerge clearly when sediments on the inner continental shelves are examined (Table 4.1).

Sources of coastal sediment

A popular misconception is that the bulk of coastal sediment is produced by the erosion of marine cliffs. In reality, coastal cliff erosion contributes only a small amount of sediment to present coasts. The bulk of the sediment comes from fluvial erosion of the continents and wave

Table 4.1 The relationship of coastal climate and sediments on the inner continental shelf.

Coastal climatic zone	Known bottom sediments (%)						Unknown %
	Rocky	Gravel	Coral	Shell	Sand	Mud	
Rainy tropical	3.2	0.3	12.3	4.4	31.4	48.5	21.2
Subhumid tropical	5.2	1.4	13.5	4.5	38.4	37.0	15.8
Warm semi-arid	3.7	–	8.6	4.2	59.5	24.0	8.5
Warm arid	4.4	–	7.3	4.8	52.1	31.4	24.2
Hyper-arid	9.1	0.6	20.9	12.0	44.5	12.8	33.6
Rainy subtropical	11.7	0.4	3.8	6.6	54.3	23.2	5.4
Summer-dry subtropical	26.1	4.1	2.1	2.7	37.3	27.7	11.9
Rainy marine	26.2	–	2.4	2.4	63.3	5.7	30.0
Wet-winter temperate	29.7	6.3	–	1.6	53.6	8.9	8.6
Rainy temperate	18.6	9.1	–	4.8	48.2	19.2	4.8
Cool semi-arid	–	–	–	7.1	92.9	–	–
Cool arid	20.2	4.8	2.4	3.6	52.8	16.3	20.8
Subpolar	30.8	14.9	–	3.5	39.3	11.5	7.0
Polar	20.8	16.2	–	4.8	43.1	15.1	9.2
Total known bottom sediments	13.3	4.1	6.4	4.8	43.5	28.0	–

Source: Hayes (1967).

transport from the sea floor (Fig. 4.1). There are great variations in the amount of sediment derived directly from erosion of cliffs. For example, the 15 m high till cliffs of Holderness in Humberside retreat at 1–2 m per year and some 30 per cent of the till sediments remain on the beach. On the other hand, many hard rock cliffs in the west of the British Isles erode slowly and contribute little sediment to beaches (see Fig. 3.1). In spite of this variability, the sediment produced by the erosion of cliffs accounts for less than 0.1 per cent of the sediment supplied by rivers.

Fluvial erosion of the continents is by far the most important source of coastal sediment, supplying over 90 per cent of global marine sediment. Glaciers and biological activity supply most of the remainder. Again, there are large spatial variations in the importance of such supply. In low latitudes, fluvial supply is dominant whereas in mid latitudes rivers carry less sediment. In high latitude areas such as Iceland, fluvial supply may dominate because of the large sediment loads of glacial streams.

The principal remaining source of beach sediment is the offshore zone since shoaling waves move sediment towards the coast within depths of $L_o/4$. However, it seems that only in depths of less than approximately 20 m are *substantial* volumes of sediment moved. In the past, glaciers and rivers deposited sediment in the offshore zone of mid latitudes and it is this sediment that has moved onshore. Many of the beaches of the northern and western isles of Scotland are composed almost entirely of shells derived from the shallow offshore shelf. In several areas of the world there is mounting evidence to indicate that the offshore source of sediment is no longer as important to coasts as it has been in the past. The decline in sediment supply from offshore is one of the reasons for the widespread occurrence of eroding coasts, for example in much of north-west Europe and north America.

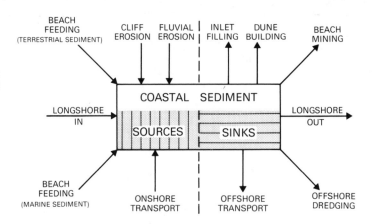

Fig. 4.1 Sources and sinks of coastal sediment can be quantified to produce a sediment budget. Note the human element in the coastal sediment budget. Source: modified from Davies (1980).

Sinks of coastal sediment

Sediment is lost from the coastal system into the major sediment sinks of dune building, inlet filling and offshore transport (Fig. 4.1). On many world coasts any excess sediment that accumulates at the back of the beach is blown into sand dunes which extend inland. Developing sand dunes are an index of healthy beaches with plentiful sediment. Once the sand reaches a position where it can no longer be acted upon by storm waves it is lost to the beach system.

Inlet filling is a major sediment sink since most estuaries and inlets are filled with fluvial or coastal sediment that would otherwise be available for beach building. When the inlet becomes totally filled it ceases to be an active sink. The Wash, in eastern England, is a good example of a rapidly filling sediment sink.

Sediment loss to the offshore zone occurs during storm conditions and in most circumstances such sediment is moved slowly onshore again by fair-weather waves. However, permanent loss occurs where the frequency of storms is such that more sediment moves offshore than is replaced by onshore movement. In areas where there is deep water close inshore, sediments may be lost down submarine coastal slopes or submarine canyons.

Coastal sediment cells

The longshore transport of material is both a source and a sink of sediment. If more sediment is moved out of a bay than is moved in, then erosion is likely. Thus longshore transport represents a redistribution of sediment that is already within the coastal system. Because interchange of sediments exists between parts of the coast, it is useful to think in terms of coastal sediment cells or compartments within which it is possible to quantify the amount of sediment gained from sources and lost to sinks, and so derive a beach sediment budget. Taken over several years, beach sediment budgets can highlight variations in the amount of source and sink sediments. As such they are an invaluable tool for assessing the causes of coastal change, e.g. the effect of artificial coastal structures on beach erosion.

Beaches

Beaches are accumulations of sediment deposited by waves and currents in the shore zone. The seaward limit of the beach roughly

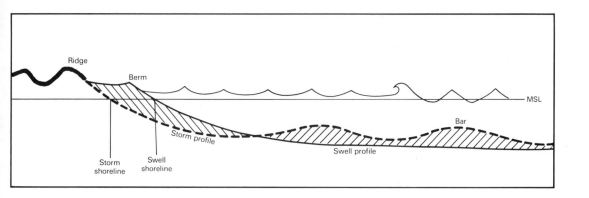

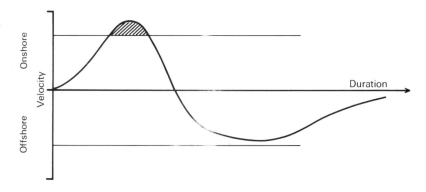

Fig. 4.2 Beach profile variability. Storm profiles are generally of lower gradient than swell profiles owing to net sediment movement offshore. Note the migration of the shoreline landwards when the storm profile develops.

Fig. 4.3 Wave velocity asymmetry in the nearshore zone. In this example onshore wave velocity reaches a critical value sufficient to move a given particle, but offshore velocity does not. The particle moves onshore. Source: modified from Komar (1976).

corresponds to the start of wave transformation and sediment movement in water shallower than $L_o/4$, so the limit will vary depending on wave and tide conditions. The landward limit of the beach is the limit of wave action. Coastal sand dunes are not included unless they are affected by waves (see Fig. 1.5).

Beach profile

Waves and the profile   Beach profiles are highly variable and subject to frequent changes depending on wave, tide and sediment characteristics. It is useful to consider two extremes of beach profile: *storm* (or *cut*) profiles and *swell* (or *fill*) profiles. These extremes should not be interpreted as seasonal profiles unless there is distinct seasonality in the regional wave climate; in Britain, storm profiles can occur at any time of the year. Under storm conditions, the waves tend to be high and steep and this removes material from a sandy beach to deposit it offshore in bars parallel to the shore. In contrast, under swell wave conditions (in fair weather), the waves are low and flat, leading to sand movement onshore to form a wide *berm* or ridge on the upper profile (Fig. 4.2).

Of the mechanisms proposed to account for these profile changes, the one that has gained most widespread support relates to the asymmetry of water velocities in the onshore and offshore directions (Fig. 4.3). In storm conditions, with high and steep waves, both the onshore and offshore velocities exceed the velocity required to move sediment. Since the offshore velocities are of longer duration than the onshore velocities, sediment will move in a net offshore direction. Sediment is cut from the upper beach leading to a reduction in overall beach gradient (Fig. 4.2). Conversely, in swell conditions, only the high magnitude onshore velocity is capable of moving sediment and so the

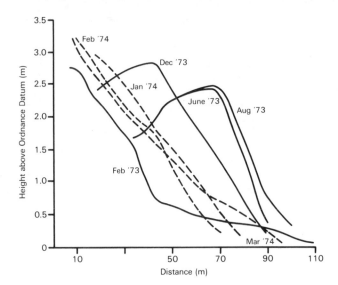

Fig. 4.4 Beach profile changes on Aberdeen Beach, Grampian. Source: Buchan and Ritchie (1979).

movement is onshore. Sediment fills the upper beach, leading to an increase in overall beach gradient (Fig. 4.2). Variations in the beach at Aberdeen Bay, Grampian (see Fig. 1.1), clearly show this very common cycle. In the summer months of 1973, the surveyed profiles showed accretion and steepening of the beach (Fig. 4.4). Erosion of the beach between August and December 1973 continued into the winter months of 1974, together with a reduction in beach gradient.

One implication of the cut and fill cycle is that the volume of beach sediment remains in a relatively constant or equilibrium state fluctuating in response to wave conditions; sediment that is rapidly cut during a storm is slowly replaced during fair weather. A second implication is that the cut of the upper beach leads to a landward movement of the shoreline and fill leads to a seaward shift. Over time any imbalance in the cut and fill cycle leads to shoreline erosion or progradation.

Sediment and the profile   The above explanation of profile changes assumes a constant sediment size on the beach, yet on many beaches there may be a considerable size range of sediments and this influences beach profiles in two ways. First, under storm conditions coarser sediments are moved only by the higher onshore velocities and not by the lower offshore velocities, so the sediment becomes coarser landwards. As a result of the size-sorting of sediments the profile becomes concave upwards because the coarser sediment higher up rests at steeper angles. Second, beach sediment size influences the backwash by controlling the amount of water lost through percolation into the beach face. On pebble beaches, the rate of percolation is higher than on sandy beaches, backwash is reduced and the slopes are steeper (Fig. 4.5).

Sediment size also influences the height of the beach crest. The height of sandy beaches is governed by the limit of swash but pebbles may be thrown well beyond the swash limit resulting in pebble storm ridges several metres above high water mark. The action of plunging breakers can throw individual pebbles considerable distances but it also seems likely that overtopping of pebble ridges occurs under surging waves

Fig. 4.5 A steep pebble beach in Spey Bay, Grampian. Large amounts of coarse beach sediments have been supplied in the past from the nearby River Spey.

Fig. 4.6 Chesil Beach, Dorset is a form of barrier beach that has migrated onshore owing to a rising sea-level. A long lagoon called The Fleet has been impounded behind the beach. The beach displays notoriously excellent longshore sediment sorting. At the eastern end (foreground), the median pebble size is 6 cm. From here, there is an almost perfect steady decline in sediment size with distance until at the western end, some 28 km downcoast, the size has decreased to pea-sized grains with a large proportion of sand.

which carry pebbles to altitude; Chesil Beach in Dorset reaches 13 m above high water mark (Fig. 4.6).

In addition to size sorting of sediments across the profile, some stretches of beach show longshore size sorting of sediments. Longshore sorting can be produced in three principal ways:

1 Selective transport rates under oblique waves can result in pronounced longshore sorting. Commonly the finer particles outdistance the coarser ones, which remain closer to the source area. Downdrift fining of sediments occurs in Bridgwater Bay, Somerset.
2 Sorting alongshore may be achieved by selective removal of finer grains from the beach by waves. The further the sediment travels, the more fines are removed and the coarser the beach becomes. The downdrift coarsening of beaches in East Anglia has been interpreted in this way.
3 Longshore variations in wave energy lead to size sorting alongshore as finer sediments accumulate in low energy areas and coarsest sediments are found in exposed areas. At Chesil Beach, where excellent longshore sorting is found, the coarsest pebbles are found where the offshore slope is steepest and wave energy is highest (Fig. 4.6).

No new sediment is added to Chesil Beach and so the longshore sorting is good. Where new sediment is added to the beach by cliff erosion, for example, longshore sorting is poor owing to the constant addition of unsorted sediments. Good longshore sorting is the exception rather than the rule and most of Britain's beaches display only poor or partially developed longshore sorting.

Tides and the profile   Strong tidal currents exist in macro-tidal environments which may move sediment towards beaches, especially near river mouths and bays. An extremely important tidal effect is the extent to which the breaker and swash zones are forced to migrate with fluctuating water levels. A large tidal range results in wave processes being spread across a great horizontal and vertical distance; a low tidal range (below 2m) results in the concentration of wave processes and the subsequent development of a single prominent beach ridge. Where tidal range is greater, the well-developed high water mark ridge is matched by a ridge at low water mark, presumably because these two levels are where swash action is most prolonged in the tidal cycle. These so-called 'high-tide' and 'low-tide' beaches are often separated by a wide, shallow 'low-tide terrace' that may be crossed by several shore-parallel *ridges* separated by low areas called *runnels*. Generally, the high-tide beach is composed of coarser sediments than the low-tide terrace, and the junction can be rather abrupt, as at Borth, Dyfed (Fig. 4.7).

In Chapter 2 it was suggested that global storm wave and swell wave environments could be identified. From the above discussion, beach profiles show differences that are strongly related to variations in waves with profile filling under swell waves and profile cutting under storm waves. Such broad patterns suggest that low-latitude, swell-dominated coasts are conducive to the development of large beach systems, while on mid-latitude, high wave energy coasts, beaches are much less extensive.

Beach plan

Beach plan or longshore shape depends mainly on the coastal outline and the wave conditions. Some open coast beaches are long and straight

Fig. 4.7 A flat low-tide terrace of sand and a steep high-tide beach of pebbles at Borth, Dyfed. The patches of peat and tree stumps on the foreshore are the eroded remnants of forest now inundated by sea-level rise (see Chapter 7).

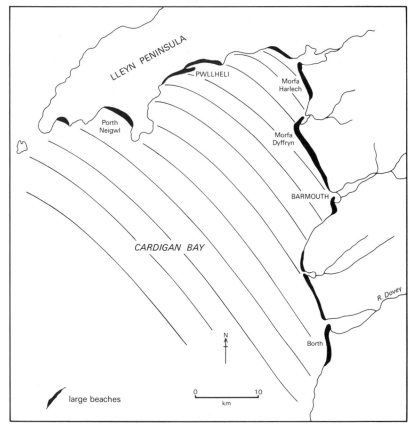

Fig. 4.8 Swash-aligned beaches in Cardigan Bay, Dyfed. The beaches have adjusted to face the predominant south-westerly wave direction. The hypothetical wave refraction patterns shown give an impression of how the beaches have adjusted to fit the waves by sediment movement and beach rotation. The adjacent rocky coast remains unadjusted to the wave crests.

whereas others are small and tightly curved, especially in bays on indented coastlines. Another type of beach may actually be detached from the mainland itself as in the case of the barrier beaches off the east coast of the United States.

Changes in beach plan are dominated by the longshore movement of sediment driven by currents related to the oblique approach of waves. The two basic types of beach plan are controlled by the angle of

Fig. 4.9 Intertidal groynes built at right-angles to the beach interrupt longshore sediment transport. The updrift beach builds seawards whilst the sediment-starved downdrift beach lowers and recedes.

incidence of these waves on the shore. Where the waves are perfectly refracted, the wave crests are parallel to the beach and no longshore current is possible. This *swash alignment* is common on indented coastlines where longshore sediment movement is limited. Small shifts in the direction of wave approach create small shifts in plan and the beach swivels about its axis. There are good examples of swash alignment in Cardigan Bay, Dyfed (Fig. 4.8).

Where the waves persistently approach the beach at an oblique angle, the longshore current continually moves sediment alongshore, removing it from the updrift section and depositing it downdrift. The longshore movement is best seen where it has been interrupted by groynes or jetties built across its path (Fig. 4.9). This *drift alignment* is common on open coastlines like that of eastern England. At advanced stages in their development some drift-aligned features, such as spits, undergo erosion of their updrift section and deposition on their downdrift sections (Fig. 4.10 a,b). The beach plan then rotates through time from drift alignment to swash alignment, with the attendant danger of breaching of the eroding updrift neck of the spit.

To some extent it appears that all beaches must develop from drift alignment towards swash alignment, although the rates of adjustment vary enormously. Small pocket beaches achieve the equilibrium condition of swash alignment rapidly; some open coast beaches may never attain it.

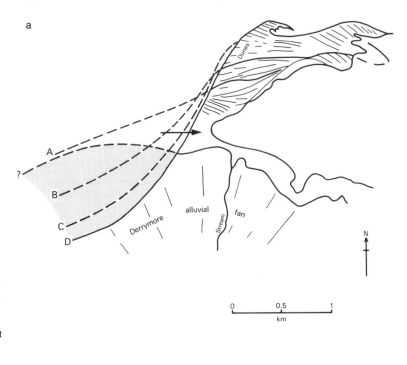

a

Fig. 4.10(a) The updrift erosion and downdrift deposition at Derrynane Spit in Co. Kerry, Ireland has led to swivelling of the spit from drift alignment (A) towards swash alignment (D). The sediments are deposited in pebble ridges whose orientation is related to the shoreline position at the time of deposition. Ongoing erosion may truncate these ridges and ultimately breach the neck of the spit (position indicated by an arrow). Source: King (1972).

(b) This 5m-long spit has adjusted to waves approaching from the left of the photograph in a tidal lagoon near Vik in southern Iceland. The outlines of previous spits can be seen in the foreground as well as the finger-like recurves caused by wave refraction and sediment transport around the tip of the spit.

| ~~~ Shingle ridges | ?----- Eroded section of alluvial fan | A---- Estimated positions of previous spits |

b

Large-scale depositional forms

Most coastal deposition serves to straighten an originally irregular shoreline; however, some deposition creates irregularities and prominences. Sites characterised by long-term deposition tend to develop large and often spectacular features. For example, on an indented coast, ongoing deposition tends to add swash-aligned berms to the original beach face and a wide coastal plain develops. The Morrich More, in the Dornoch Firth, Highland, has developed in this way over the last 6,000 years or so with successive sand ridges building seawards

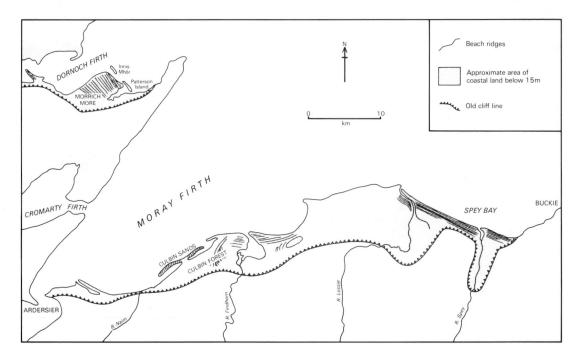

Fig. 4.11 Coastal deposition, mainly over the last 6,000 years or so, has resulted in the seaward migration of the Moray Firth coast in Scotland. Together with a slow uplift of the land (see Chapter 7), coastal deposition has infilled much of the area seawards of the 15 m contour, resulting in a smooth coastal outline.

to create some 22 km^2 of deposition. The most recent additions to the feature are the two small sandy islands of Innis Mhór and Patterson Island (Fig. 4.11). Further south in the Moray Firth the coastline between Ardersier and Buckie has been gradually infilled with vast amounts of sediments washed down the rivers Nairn, Findhorn, Lossie and Spey to produce a broad, smooth coastal outline (Fig. 4.11). On the south coast of the Moray Firth the direction of wave approach is commonly from the east or north-east, so longshore currents are responsible for the westward transport of coarse sands and pebbles brought down by the rivers. Many coasts are subject to similar amounts of sediment input and the resultant deposition allows building out of the coast to occur in the form of spits, tombolos, forelands, barrier islands and deltas.

Spits

Spits are large, narrow accumulations of beach sediment with one end attached to the mainland and the other projecting into the sea or into a large lake (Fig. 4.10 a,b). They occur as a result of longshore sediment transport beyond an abrupt change in coastal orientation and are thus common at river exits and estuaries and on indented coasts. The change in orientation results in a reduction of the longshore current, and sediment deposition at this point extends the spit feature in the current direction. Finer sediments accumulate in the sheltered area in the lee of the spit, leading to mudflat and salt marsh development. Characteristic of many spits are the finger-like recurves or hooks at the downdrift end (see Fig. 4.10b). These are thought to be due to sediment reworking by waves arriving from different directions and to wave refraction around the tip of the spit. In locations where the spit extends across a river exit, ongoing deposition can lead to the downdrift deflection of the river itself. This is most common where small rivers enter the sea or where the longshore currents are particularly strong. Orford Ness in Suffolk extends for almost 15 km and has deflected the River Ore southwards from its original exit at Slaughden. The northern section between

Fig. 4.12 Orford Ness: spit
extension in the direction of
longshore drift. Source: Carr
(1972).

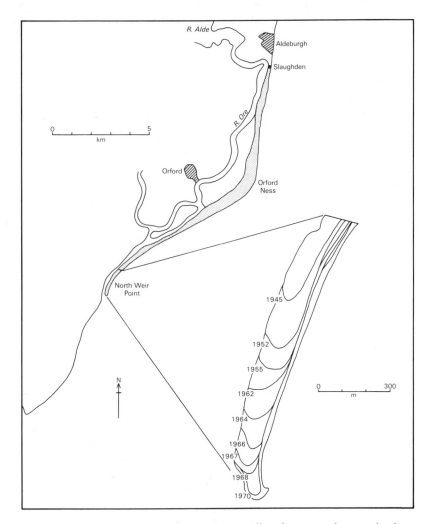

Aldeburgh and Orford Ness has been eroding for several centuries but
the southern section at North Weir Point shows southward growth over
recent decades (Fig. 4.12). This highlights another characteristic of
spits. Extension of the spit requires an ongoing supply of sediment from
the updrift section of coast and this may lead to erosion of the updrift
part of the spit itself. Through time, updrift erosion and downdrift
deposition may lead to rotation of the original drift-aligned spit towards
swash alignment (see Fig. 4.10a). The former orientation of many
British spits can be deduced from the orientation of old shingle ridges
truncated by updrift erosion. Depending on the nature of the coast to
which a spit is attached, it may undergo cyclic development. For
example, the development and decay of successive spits at Spurn Point
in Humberside are directly linked to the erosion of the glacial till cliffs
to which the spit is attached. By the time Spurn Point has extended
some way into the Humber estuary, coastal erosion of the till root has
exposed the thin updrift neck of the spit. When this is breached in storm
conditions, a new spit develops to the north-west of the earlier one (Fig.
4.13). Since the end of the nineteenth century, the neck of Spurn has
been artificially protected and as it becomes more and more exposed
because of ongoing updrift erosion, the likelihood of a major breach
increases. It is due to Spurn's key position at the entrance to the
Humber that detailed references to it and to the ports and lighthouses

49

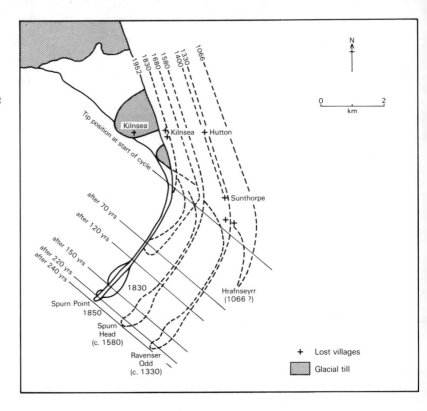

Fig. 4.13 The cyclical development of Spurn Point and its predecessors is linked to the ongoing erosion and retreat of the glacial till cliffs. As the till root moves westward so the spit becomes exposed, its narrow neck is breached and the spit is destroyed. A new spit subsequently develops to the north-west. Source: de Boer (1964).

that stood on its predecessors are so frequent in old manuscripts, maps and records dating back to AD 657. This information together with the remnants of the previous spits are the basic ingredients in the cyclic model shown in Fig. 4.13. It is this key position that now causes most concern, for if the neck of the Spurn were to be breached, the effects on the navigable channels of the Humber would be difficult to predict and the long-term future of the coastal navigation and lifeboat installations now at the point would be in jeopardy.

Spits are by far the most important depositional features jutting out from the coast. Where they connect an island to the mainland the term *tombolo* is generally used. More commonly tombolos form in the wave shadow of an offshore island, the resultant deposition creating a thin neck of sediment which eventually extends to the mainland. In the British Isles the best examples of tombolos are found on the indented coastlines of south-west Ireland and the western and northern isles of Scotland.

Cuspate forelands

Most of the coastal features mentioned so far tend to smooth and straighten the coastline. Cuspate forelands, however, create large irregularities on the coast as a result of wave refraction around offshore shoals or islands, or of restricted wave approach directions. Cuspate forelands are roughly triangular projections from the coast and can grow to a considerable size; the Carolina Capes on the east coast of the USA are each about 150–200 km long. Cape Hatteras, Cape Fear and Cape Canaveral all have offshore shoal complexes which allow deposition in their lee in addition to longshore transport of sediment from nearby rivers. One of the best documented cuspate forelands is

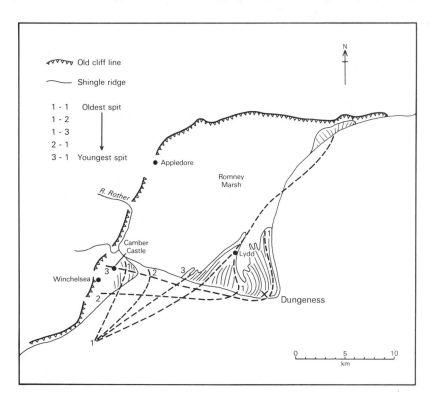

Fig. 4.14 Foreland evolution: the downdrift extension of a spit across a formerly wide and shallow bay, at the present site of the Romney Marsh in Kent, heralded the beginnings of Dungeness foreland. Over time, updrift erosion and downdrift deposition of the spit led to rotation of the feature from alignment 1 to alignment 3. The central tidal marshland of Dungeness was probably reclaimed in two phases: in the north Romney Marsh was drained during the Roman period; whilst the thirteenth-century diversion of the River Rother from its course north of Lydd to its new exit north of Camber Castle led to the draining of the southern marshes. The location of a nuclear power station, on an eroding shoreline, is marked 'X'. Source: Steers (1946).

the 250 km^2 of shingle ridge and reclaimed marsh of Dungeness in Kent. No offshore shoals exist here but the location of its sharp point may be due to the proximity of the French coast which limits the approach of south-east waves. The development of Dungeness relates to the downdrift extension under south-west waves of a spit from the south across a wide, cliff-backed bay (Fig. 4.14). Shingle transported from the eroding updrift end was deposited downdrift leading to migration to the north-east as well as rotation seawards. Despite ongoing erosion of the south flank under south-west waves and deposition on the eastern flank under north-east waves, Dungeness is a good example of the evolution of drift alignment towards swash alignment. Historical records provide a fascinating insight into the human consequences of coastal deposition. In AD 893 the Danes sailed past Lydd to Appledore with a fleet of 250 vessels (Fig. 4.14). Later, in 1292, King Henry I completed the new port of Winchelsea but the accumulation of new shingle ridges soon isolated it from the sea. Winchelsea's coastal replacement, Camber Castle, was completed in 1539 by King Henry VIII, but by 1594 the fortification was already 244 m from the sea and by 1695 an extra 610 m of new shingle ridges had accumulated seawards of the castle.

Barrier islands and related forms

These are most common on low-gradient coasts that are subject to high wave energy and low tidal range, allowing the optimal development of wave-produced features. Barrier beaches form at the seaward edge of coastal lowland, often building well above the height of the surrounding land. Barrier islands resemble barrier beaches but are separated from the mainland by flooding of the low-lying land behind, the axis of the beach being broken by tidal channels to create a chain of offshore islands (Fig. 4.15). Three main modes of barrier formation have been

51

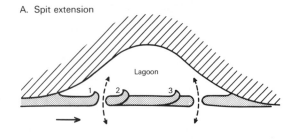

A. Spit extension

Fig. 4.15 The three modes of barrier development: lagoonal closure by longshore spit extension; onshore migration of barrier with sea-level rise; back beach flooding by sea-level rise. Chains of barrier islands have a similar form to barrier beaches but are separated by tidal channels. Source: Bird (1984).

Lagoon

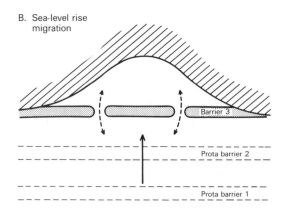

B. Sea-level rise migration

Barrier 3

Prota barrier 2

Prota barrier 1

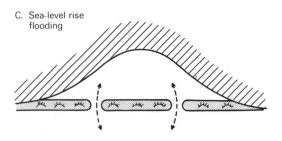

C. Sea-level rise flooding

proposed. Firstly, spits may extend alongshore to seal off a coastal bay, e.g. the barrier spits of the Baltic. Subsequent storm activity is responsible for breaching the spit to form an island chain. Secondly, beaches develop at lower sea-levels and migrate onshore, the beach keeping pace with subsequent sea-level rise but creating possible flooding behind. Chesil Beach in Dorset (Fig. 4.6) is an example of this; the process of barrier migration is still continuing owing to sea-level rise and this has led to flooding and pebble encroachment of the settlements behind the barrier. Thirdly, barrier beaches are created by sea-level rise causing flooding of the low land behind the main beach and its sand dunes. These various ideas of barrier formation are not mutually exclusive since both longshore and onshore transport of sediment may simultaneously play a role in barrier formation. There was almost certainly longshore drift of sediment on the predecessors of Chesil Beach, Dorset or Slapton Sands, Devon as they migrated landwards under a rising sea-level. The important requirement for barrier development is that sufficient sediment should be available on a low-gradient coast to allow a large beach to develop. On a global scale these conditions are best met on the trailing edge and marginal sea coasts of continents (see Chapter 1) where 76 per cent of the world's barrier systems are found.

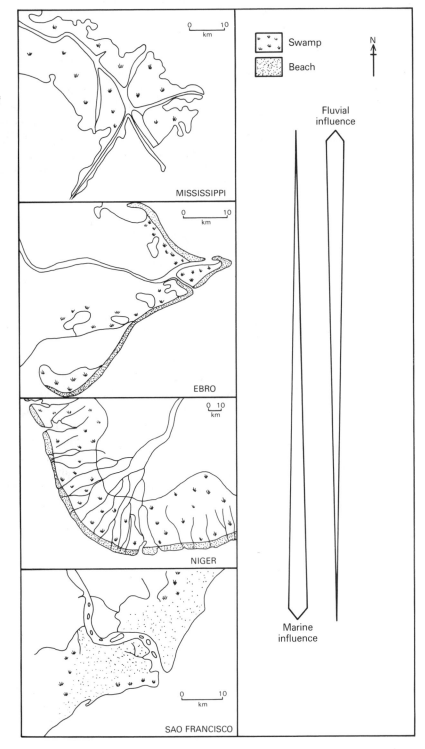

Fig. 4.16 Types of delta. Increasing marine and decreasing fluvial influences are manifest by the increasingly smooth wave-dominated coastal outline and greater occurrence of beach deposits towards the foot of the diagram. Where fluvial influences dominate, the deltaic coastline is highly indented and characterised by extensive swamps. Source: after Wright and Coleman (1972).

Deltas

These are built where fluvial sediment has infilled a river mouth or estuary to form a depositional feature which protrudes from the coast. The form of the delta depends on the relative balance between fluvial and marine processes. Where wave processes dominate, the results of fluvial deposition tend to be smoothed out and sediment moved alongshore. These *straight* or blunt deltas have outlets deflected by the construction of high, broad, sandy beaches, e.g. the deltas of the Senegal River in West Africa and the São Francisco River in Brazil (Fig. 4.16). Where fluvial processes dominate, wave action is modified by the construction of a shallow submarine platform of sediment on which is built the subaerial part of the delta. The Mississippi delta is a good example of this; the abundant sediment is delivered via long, linear channels bordered by high banks. The resultant *digitate* or birdsfoot delta is highly indented and marshy with few beaches (Fig. 4.16). Intermediate forms include the *lobate* deltas of the Niger and Nile rivers.

Depositional processes are responsible for major changes in the direction of delta growth as well as general building seawards. Extension of a channel seawards reduces the gradient and the outflow, allowing the flanking levees (banks) to be breached during floods. Since deposition in the channel, and especially on the levees where flow is slow, has raised bed and banks above the adjacent delta surface, the outflow through a breach is substantial and a new distributary channel develops rapidly. The new channel quickly extends the delta seawards in a new direction. Starved of sediment, the abandoned channel subsequently suffers erosion. Over the last 5,500 years, seven successive sub-delta areas have formed in the Mississippi delta. The present one is the furthest seaward, having been confined between artificial levees for the past 250 years, and is becoming increasingly prone to potentially dangerous flooding as its gradient declines.

On a global scale, deltas are infrequent in the temperate latitudes where fluvial sediment supply is limited and stormy conditions prevail. Deltas are most common in the low latitudes and on trailing edge coasts where large volumes of sediment are deposited on a wide continental shelf in relatively low wave energy environments.

5 Coastal sand dunes

Many depositional coastal environments are characterised by accumulations of windblown sand in the backshore zone; in Europe some 20 per cent of the coastline is backed by sand dunes. Sand dunes are much less common in the humid tropical lands, probably because of low wind velocities and continuously wet sand. There are two main types of coastal dune: vegetated and transverse. The most common type of coastal dune is *vegetated* and displays complex interactions between its vegetation and sand transport. Such dunes have irregular surfaces and dune crests that are separated by blow-outs or windswept, low channels through the dunes. Because of the presence of vegetation, these dunes develop by the deposition of low-angle beds of sand. Commonly a series of dune ridges lie parallel to the coastline (Fig. 5.1a). *Transverse* or *migrating* dunes are characterised by their lack of stabilising vegetation and in common with their desert counterparts they are highly mobile. They move landwards by high-angle slipface deposition (Fig. 5.1b) and are identifiable as large, distinct features with sinuously shaped crests. Transverse dunes can occur on most coasts but they are commonly found in the arid and semi-arid regions. The unvegetated dunes of the Sands of Forvie, Grampian are amongst Britain's few examples of this type of dune.

Factors of dune formation

Climate clearly plays a role in dune development. Subtropical, luxuriant vegetation and heavy rainfall inhibit sand movement, while an abundant sand supply, strong onshore winds and a well-adapted vegetation are important prerequisites for extensive dune development. The sand dune system can be seen as a zone of sand transit between continual movement on the wave-dominated beach and a more permanent position on land. The real interface between the marine and terrestrial systems lies in the dynamic region of upper beach and foredune, where limited wave activity allows sediment to accumulate before being carried landwards by the wind. Storm waves also readily erode this zone to reincorporate sand into the beach system proper (Fig. 5.2).

Sand supply

An abundant supply of sand grains of a calibre easily moved by winds is a requirement for dune deposition. This may be provided by large amounts of offshore sand brought onshore by tide and wave processes and in much of Europe this is the most important source. The very extensive sand dune systems or machair lands of the western isles of Scotland have high proportions of shells derived from offshore sources. Input from rivers is also important and many of the largest sand dune

Fig. 5.1(a) Vegetated sand dunes parallel to the coast at Brittas Bay, Co. Wicklow, Ireland. The youngest and lowest dunes are behind the beach where sand accumulates and is trapped by the vegetation. Two older and higher dune ridges occur landwards of this and show fairly continuous and mature vegetation cover.

(b) Transverse coastal dunes migrating landwards at up to 11 m/year engulf vegetation near Foxton, New Zealand.

a

b

systems lie close to or at the mouth of large estuaries where sand is locally abundant, e.g. Formby on the River Mersey, Merseyside, Barry Links and Tentsmuir on the Firth of Tay, Tayside and Morfa Harlech on the Dwyryd in Dyfed. In the areas where the tidal range is great, a large sand area is exposed to wind action and this enhances dune development. So too does the availability of a flat backshore area upon which dunes can develop. In many cases dunes have developed on top of raised pebble ridges that have been abandoned by the sea.

There is a delicate balance between wind direction and velocity and the formation of sand dunes. Low-velocity winds do not move the sand, whereas extreme velocities tend to destroy dunes, and it is probable that the more frequent but less powerful prevailing winds are the most important in dune development. On a global scale, the largest dune systems are in the temperate but stormy mid latitudes and, generally, maximum dune development occurs on windward coasts. This

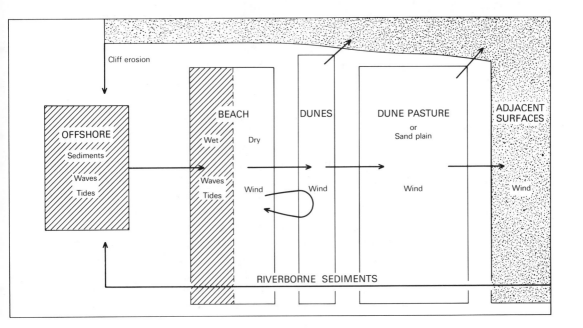

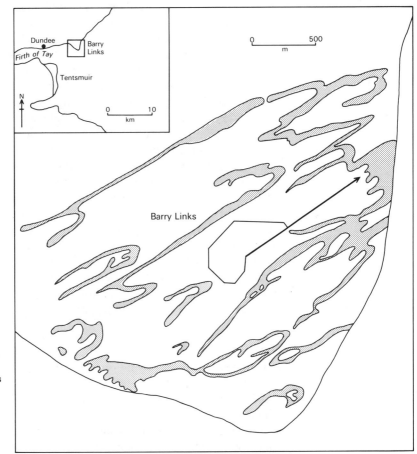

Fig. 5.2 Sand transfer system between beach and sand dune. Note the recycling of sand by wind and wave undercutting of the beach-dune interface and by fluvial incision through the system. Source: Mather and Ritchie (1977).

Fig. 5.3 The relationship between mean dune orientation and wind direction as calculated by plotting each wind direction in proportion to its sand-moving power. The resultant vector (shown by the arrow) completes the wind direction polygon and indicates the direction of dominant wind effect. The exceptionally linear nature of the dunes is caused by erosion of the central area of the dune. This creates a U-shaped or parabolic form whose vegetation-fixed flanks are parallel to the wind direction. (See p.60 and Fig. 5.7.) Source: modified from Landsberg (1956).

relationship between wind direction and dune orientation can be investigated by means of vector diagrams that take account of the relative frequency of occurrence of winds of different velocities (Fig. 5.3). Maximum dune growth occurs where the resultant vector is normal to the coast as along much of the west coast of the British Isles, e.g. Ballyheige Bay in Co. Kerry, Ireland.

Sand movement

A wind blowing over a flat beach experiences a drag effect related to the roughness of the surface layer, and very close to the ground there is a calm layer where the wind velocity drops to zero. However, some larger grains project through this layer and may begin to move when the wind velocity reaches a critical value. Grains can be entrained in one of two ways: either directly by the wind or by collision with other grains in motion. Sand transport occurs principally by saltation (about 75 per cent of total sand movement) and creep (about 25 per cent of total sand movement). Suspended grains account for a very small percentage of movement. *Saltation*, or the bouncing motion of grains, starts with grains directly entrained by the wind impacting with larger immobile grains. The impact of collision causes these larger grains to bounce up into the successively faster airstreams above. As they fall to the surface, they collide with others and soon the entire surface is saltating. Experiments show that the bigger grains bounce higher, up to 1 m above the surface, and 'get more bounce to the ounce'. Surface *creep* is caused by the impact of saltating grains on the grains too large to be bounced up. These larger grains jerk forward as the saltating ones impact and this slow process results in substantial movement. The effect of moisture on sand movement is important since even low moisture contents of 1 per cent result in large increases in the velocities required to initiate movement. Again this highlights the importance of long intertidal drying times and low humidity for optimal dune development.

Because there is a fine balance between wind velocity, surface roughness, moisture content and grain size, variations in any one of these parameters leads to variations in the others. Grains saltating along a beach may reach an area where surface roughness increases, as for example at the high tide mark. The decrease in wind velocity caused by obstacles such as dried seaweed, plastic squeezy bottles and pieces of wood allows deposition to take place in a streamlined form around the obstacles. However, for deposition to continue beyond the burial of the initial obstacle, the surface roughness must be maintained and keep pace with deposition. In the natural beach system, only growing plants can perform this vital function.

The role of vegetation

Even the sparsest of vegetation can greatly increase the surface roughness and its effect is felt not only at the surface, but, due to turbulence, at some height above the ground. Experimental planting of dune grasses on a bare sand slope can increase the thickness of the calm wind layer by up to 30 times and so enhance deposition (Fig. 5.4). The first colonisers of the small mounds of sand that accumulate around the flotsam of the high water mark are generally species that are salt tolerant like sand twitch (*Agropyron junceiforme*) and, to a lesser extent, sea lyme grass (*Elymus arenaria*). These grow as sand deposition proceeds, their foliage creating even more deposition and their root networks binding the sand together into low *embryo dunes* (Fig. 5.5). Other colonising species of backshore and embryo dunes are

Fig. 5.4 The presence of vegetation on an embryo dune greatly enhances the sand deposition rate. Rapid deposition encourages and stimulates plant growth and the sand dune grows in size.

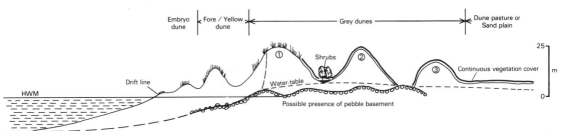

Fig. 5.5 A typical dune system developed under conditions of continuous sand supply from the beach. As the embryo dunes grow into larger 'yellow' dunes, new embryo dunes develop to seaward. Reduction of sand supply due to the growth of these developing dunes eventually results in vegetation stabilisation of the older dunes. Although marram still dominates the first dune ridge, the second, third and subsequent dune ridges are grass- and moss-covered.

Many dune systems in the British Isles have been deposited on top of old pebble ridges in the backshore and these may be re-exposed if the beach subsequently begins to erode and removes the younger dunes (shown by the dashed line).

the annuals sea rocket (*Cakile maritima*) and prickly saltwort (*Salsoli kali*).

As the embryo dunes grow in height, they coalesce laterally to form a *foredune ridge* parallel to the shoreline. Elevation of the dune above the level of occasional inundation allows species that are adapted to the dry, less saline conditions to colonise. The most vigorous of these is marram grass (*Ammophila arenaria*). Its ability to extend rhizomes or shoots both horizontally and vertically means that it is perfectly equipped to cope with deposition rates of up to 1 m of sand per year. In fact the growth and vigour of marram is directly related to the rate of influx of sand. As they grow, such foredunes are often called *yellow dunes* on account of the amount of bare sand yet to be colonised. However, the effect of vegetation cover on sand deposition means that these dunes grow rapidly in height from modest 1–2 m foredunes into dunes about 10 m high.

Landwards of the foredune ridge, the increasing amount of vegetation and the presence of dunes to seaward mean that sand movement is more restricted. However, because the dunes are higher, wind velocities are greater close to the windward crest, leading to sand movement over the crest and deposition in the lee. The dune therefore builds upwards and landwards until it reaches a height where the stronger winds remove as much as they deposit. Thus this *first dune ridge* may achieve heights of 15–30 m and because sand is still mobile, the dominant species is marram, although grasses such as red fescue (*Festuca rubra*) and sand sedge (*Carex arenaria*) invade.

59

Landwards of this first dune ridge, there may be several dune ridges separated by damp slacks (see Fig. 5.1a). Sand supply is by now negligible and these older or *grey dunes* are characterised by dieback of the once vigorous marram and invasion by grey-coloured lichens of the genus *Cladonia*, along with mosses, grasses and low shrubs such as sea buckthorn (*Hippophae rhamnoides*).

The above developmental sequence takes place not only in time but in space: as the foredunes are building upwards, new embryo dunes are developing on the shoreline. Even the oldest grey dunes, now several dune ridges inland, began as embryo dunes close to the high water mark. This is an important point because the crucial requirement for sand dune development is an ongoing sand supply to fuel either the addition of dune ridges seawards or the slow migration of dunes landwards. There are also vegetational and soil changes taking place over time in the dune system. As the influence of salt and mobile sand decreases inland, so different species invade and become dominant (Fig. 5.6), their presence increasing the amount of decaying vegetation and the organic and moisture content of the developing soil. Lime content also decreases landwards as any beach shells present are leached away.

However, the sequence of sand dune development and its associated vegetation is not yet complete, for within the developing systems shown in Figs. 5.5 and 5.6 is an erosional subsystem.

Factors of dune erosion

Virtually all dune systems are subject to erosion. The most common type of erosion is *point erosion* or blow-out development. Dune systems do not develop in splendid isolation for any destruction of the fragile vegetation cover leads to renewed sand movement. Commonly rabbits dig burrows and graze the vegetation of many of our largest dune systems – one has only to recall the names Newborough Warren in Anglesey and Braunton Burrows and Dawlish Warren in Devon to realise that! Such destruction of the vegetation cover by animals or by the wearing of paths through the ridges may begin early in the dune sequence, but it is in the older grey dunes and dune pasture that the effects become most noticeable. Wind gains access to the sand beneath the vegetation cover, often close to the ridge crests, and very rapidly erodes the surface, causing a depression or blow-out. As the wind is channelled into it the blow-out grows, the eroded sand inundating adjacent surfaces whose plants are ill-equipped to cope with sand deposition. Removal of sand from the blow-out and deposition of this sand downwind results in the development of a U-shaped or *parabolic dune* whose long arms (the sides of the old dune) are separated by a large, deflated blow-out (Figs. 5.3, 5.7). The blow-out will expand laterally until its width reduces the channelling effect of the wind and vertically until it reaches the water table or pebble basement, as occurs in the Ynyslas dunes in Dyfed. The adjacent grey dune surfaces, however, are suddenly revitalised as clumps of previously moribund marram grass now grow vigorously in the new 'foredune' environment (Fig. 5.7). There are large parabolic dunes at Rattray Head in the

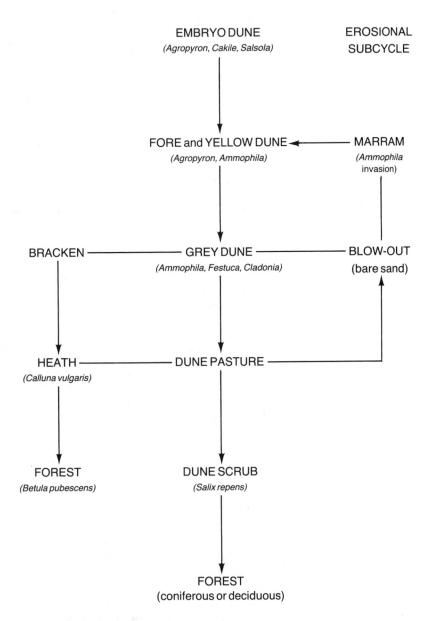

Fig. 5.6 Dune development cycle and vegetation. On acid soils, heath may develop to birchwood as on Walney Island, in Cumbria. The great bulk of British dunes terminate as either grassland or heath and most go through an erosional subcycle of blow-out development and restabilisation. Source: Chapman (1976).

Grampian region, at Kenfig Burrows in west Glamorgan and in many other dune systems. The net effect of this erosion of grey dune systems is the general lowering of dune morphology, destruction of ridge orientation and replacement by an amorphous, low-lying and rolling *dune pasture* or *sandplain*. These often provide the basis for excellent golf courses such as at Carnoustie Links in Tayside, St Andrews Links in Fife and at Royal Lytham St Annes in Lancashire. On the west coast of Scotland and in the western isles, the sand plains or machair lands are very extensive and form an important grazing area for the livestock of crofters.

Fig. 5.7 Point erosion in the form of a large blow-out in grey dunes at Morfa Harlech, Dyfed. The downward growth of the blow-out has been arrested by the presence of a water-table. Adjacent mature dune vegetation has been inundated and moribund marram revitalised by newly deposited sand blown from the blow-out.

Fig. 5.8 Frontal erosion of grey dunes at White Strand, Co. Clare, Ireland may be caused by a combination of slow sea-level rise and reduction in sand supply. Note the occurrence of blow-outs along the line of dunes. Dune stabilisation schemes have proved successful where blow-outs occur but widespread frontal erosion poses a more serious problem for dune management.

The second type of dune erosion is *frontal erosion* where the entire seaward face of the dune system retreats, often as a marked cliff line (Fig. 5.8). Such erosion begins at the drift line and embryo dune and eventually, in time, removes foredunes and grey dunes. The cause of frontal erosion may be an increase in wave energy on the beach resulting from a slow sea-level rise or a reduction in sediment supply, or both. There is now substantial evidence to suggest that the sediment supplies from offshore that were formerly so plentiful are now much reduced. Such a reduction affects the beach sediment budget and reduces the amount of surplus sand available to be blown into sand dunes. The shoreline moves landwards into the dune system, leading to a familiar crest-line retreat of old dunes separated from the high water mark by a steep 30° slope of loose sand and slipping clumps of crestal vegetation. In much of western Europe and especially in the west and north of Britain, this erosional sequence in dunes is common. Because loose sand slopes occur along the entire length of these eroding dune systems, conditions are now ideal for *point erosion* to proceed and the frontal cliff becomes punctured with large blow-outs. Only where the sediment supply is locally enhanced at river exits or by longshore drift is a full developing dune sequence found in Britain; elsewhere the sequence is erosional.

6 Estuaries

Estuaries are the lower courses of river valleys which are now flooded by the sea and through which the river still flows. There is considerable overlap in this definition with that of *rias* which are drowned river valleys (see Fig. 2.1a) and *fjords* and *firths* which are drowned glacial valleys. Both of these categories of drowned valley may still have significant fluvial input and so may be estuarine in character. Others may be little more than inlets of the sea with no fluvial input. Perhaps the ideal estuary is long and funnel-shaped, like the Thames estuary in south-east England, within which mixing of fresh and salt water takes place. There is considerable variation in estuary form as well as in the amount of mixing that takes place. In addition, estuaries provide sheltered environments within which deposition of fine sediment takes place in such large quantities that extensive tidal flats and salt marshes dominate the inner reaches and naturally reclaim land from the sea.

Estuarine processes

Processes in estuaries are mainly controlled by the interaction of tidal and non-tidal currents.

Tidal currents

As the tidal wave advances into a shallowing estuary it becomes increasingly asymmetric as frictional effects begin to steepen the crest of the wave or *flood* tide and flatten the trough or *ebb*. The flood tide shortens in duration to two or three hours and the ebb lengthens to eight or nine hours of the 12.4-hour tidal cycle. The change in the tidal wave may be so marked that it becomes a *bore* where the gradient of the estuary increases landwards. The bores in the rivers Severn and Trent in England, for example, are well known. At the northern end of the Bay of Fundy, in eastern Canada, the bore in the River Petitcodiac consists of a steep 5 m-high wave whose roar can be heard 20 km away! Such increased flood velocities serve to move more sediment *into* estuaries than is carried out. Estuaries are thus sediment sinks, trapping sediment from the outer coast; for example, some 26,000 hectares of marshland have been gained by estuarine deposition in the Wash, eastern England, over the past 1,700 years. The differences in velocities encourage the flood and ebb to take different paths or channels through the estuary and these velocity differences are one of the keys to estuarine deposition. The highest velocities in an estuary occur at mid-tide when the channels are only partially filled and the lowest velocities occur close to high tide when the water spills out of the channels over the adjacent mudflats. Thus the rate of deposition outside the channels is rapid, since they are flooded twice daily by slow-moving,

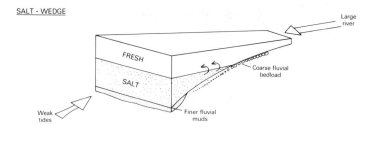

Fig. 6.1   Types of estuary: salt-wedge estuaries are dominated by strong river outflows leading to vertical flow separation; partially mixed estuaries are subject to strong tidal flows leading to mixing of fresh and salt water; fully mixed estuaries tend to be wide, leading to lateral flow separation. Source: Pethick (1984).

PARTIALLY MIXED

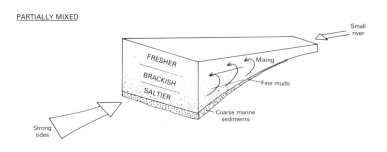

FULLY MIXED

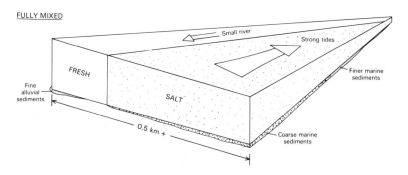

sediment-laden water. The channels are swept clean of sediments by higher water velocities.

Non-tidal currents

These are set up by the mixing of fresh and salt water. As fresh water is less dense than salt, it rises above the salt water, the degree of mixing being controlled by the relative amounts and velocities of the two opposing flows. Three types of estuarine circulation have been identified:

1   *Salt-wedge estuaries* are fluvially dominated estuaries with weak marine inflow due to a small tidal range. Salt water forms a tapering wedge (Fig. 6.1) beneath the fresh water which rises at the tip and deposits its coarser sediments. Finer sediments are deposited seawards and so this type of estuary has mainly fluvial sediments coarsening landwards. Depending on the volume of sediment deposited, the estuary may develop into a delta; the Mississippi is a good example of a salt-wedge estuary.
2   *Partially-mixed estuaries* occur where a large tidal range and a low river discharge result in pronounced mixing of fresh and salt water, although there is a crude density-based stratification from saltier bottom water through brackish to fresher water on top (Fig. 6.1).

Fig. 6.2 Marine sands near Burntisland on the north bank of the Firth of Forth in Scotland. Fully mixed estuaries such as the Forth tend to have one bank dominated by marine water and sediments (in this case, the north bank) and the other dominated by fluvial water and sediments.

Strong tidal flow means that marine sediments are moved into the estuary, fining landwards as the velocities decrease. The River Thames in southern England is a good example of this.

3 *Fully mixed estuaries* are generally wider than about 0.5 km with strong tidal flows and a fairly weak river flow. They show little vertical mixing but the two flows are separated laterally. In the northern hemisphere the Coriolis force, caused by the earth's rotation, swings water flow to the right. Facing inland, this means that the tidal flow is deflected to the right bank of the wide estuary and the seaward-moving river flows on the left (Fig. 6.1). The Firth of Forth in Scotland is a good example of this: powerful tides sweep marine sands onto the north (right) bank of the estuary and fluvial sediments dominate on the south (left) bank (Fig. 6.2).

Estuarine form

Because estuarine processes are dominated by tidal range, it follows that the general form of estuaries within a common tidal range will be similar.

1 *Micro-tidal estuaries,* where the tidal range is less than 2 m, are dominated by fluvial discharge which produces a salt-wedge circulation with deltaic sedimentation at its mouth. However, wave processes seawards of this may construct spits and barrier islands which could partially enclose the estuary, creating lagoons, as in the Gulf of Mexico.

2 *Meso-tidal estuaries* of tidal range between 2 and 4 m are subject to stronger tidal currents than micro-tidal estuaries but these tides do not extend far inland and the shape is rather truncated, often with a small flood-tide delta landwards of the mouth and an ebb-tide delta seawards of the mouth. The estuaries of the rivers Don and Ythan in the Grampian region display these features.

3 *Macro-tidal estuaries* occur in tidal ranges larger than 4 m and produce strong tidal and non-tidal currents which give rise to long,

linear sandbanks close to the seaward end. The large tidal range means that there is penetration of salt water and mixing occurs for considerable distances inland. Macro-tidal estuaries are trumpet-shaped, the decreasing width upstream being just sufficient to counteract the loss of tidal energy to bed and banks and so maintain the tidal range as it advances. Examples of macro-tidal estuaries are the Tay and Forth in Scotland and the Thames in England.

Tidal flats and salt marshes

On high energy coasts, tidal flats composed of fine sediments can only exist within sheltered inlets and estuaries. On low energy coasts, they may exist on the open coast. One of the largest tidal flats in the world is the Wadden Sea of the Netherlands where mudflats and salt marshes develop behind the protection of the Frisian Islands, a chain of offshore barrier islands (see Fig. 4.15). Tidal flats are dissected by tidal creeks up to 2m deep and are not flat but stepped both at the junction of the vegetated *high-tide flat* or *salt marsh* and the *intertidal slope* or *mud-* and *sandflat* and also at the junction of the intertidal slope and *subtidal* zone or *flood/ebb channels* (Fig. 6.3). In terms of sediment size, tidal flats are similarly varied. Mud is common on the upper tidal flat whereas muddy sediments on the intertidal slope may well become sandier, giving way to sandflats towards the low water mark. The tidal flats behind Holy Island on the Northumberland coast display this trend, the causeway linking Holy Island to the mainland providing an unusually convenient viewing platform.

Mudflats

Maximum velocities of the incoming flood tide are greatest at mid-tide levels and lowest at high tide when most deposition occurs. Further, the suspended sediment which forms the source sediment for the mudflat takes some time to settle to the bottom as high water approaches and so may travel some distance in doing so. Once settled, the sediment is not now entrained until later in the ebb flow, so it moves a shorter distance seawards than it did landwards. Deposition rates are therefore higher closer to the shoreline on the mudflat surface. The process is enhanced by the creek systems which lace the mudflat surface because they deliver water which at mid-tide is flowing fast *within* the channels. At higher tide levels the water spreads out from the creeks onto the mudflats and suffers dramatic velocity reductions. Enhanced deposition rates raise the upper mudflat surface and the number and duration of tidal inundations decline to the point where vegetation may colonise the mudflats. There are extensive sand- and mudflats in Morecambe Bay, Lancashire.

Fig. 6.3   The three geomorphological units of a tidal flat. Species zonation is well-defined on the vegetated tidal flat or salt marsh. The intertidal slopes are generally sparsely vegetated by 'meadows' of sea grasses such as *Zostera* (eel grass). Source: adapted from Davies (1980).

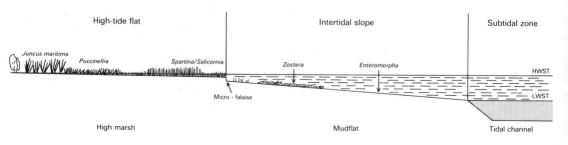

Fig. 6.4 *Spartina townsendii* (rice grass) growing on the east coast of England. The twentieth century has seen a rapid spread of *Spartina* in the British Isles from its first appearance in Southampton Water in 1870. Part of the spread is due to successful natural colonisation but planting for reclamation and stabilisation purposes is also responsible.

Salt marshes

These occupy the upper tidal flat and are generally exceptionally flat and well vegetated, though close to the junction of the upper mudflat and lower salt marsh the density of vegetation is less. Here the colonising species must be able to tolerate the highly saline and turbid water, shifting sediment and frequent cycles of submergence and exposure. The upper surfaces of the tidal flat may be partly covered and stabilised by mats of the algae *Enteromorpha*, as occurs near Tain in the Dornoch Firth. In Europe the most common colonisers of the upper tidal flats are marsh cord grass (*Spartina* spp.) and marsh samphire (*Salicornia* spp.) and these soon spread to cover much of the surface (Fig. 6.4). The presence of these plants and of the algal mat covering the mudflat surface serves to retard the tidal current during the entire period of inundation, thus allowing greater time for deposition and providing additional depositional surfaces on the vegetation itself. The result is a greatly enhanced deposition rate on the developing marsh which raises the surface and so reduces the frequency and duration of tidal inundation. The reduced flooding now creates conditions where other species may have a competitive advantage. The original colonisers are forced to extend seawards into the mudflat and the process is repeated. A well defined shore-parallel zonation of plants develops on the salt marsh, each species occupying the level of marsh most suited to its requirements (see Fig. 6.3). In Europe, the general succession is from *Salicornia* or *Spartina* on the low marsh to sea aster (*Aster maritima*) and sea purslane (*Halimione portulacoides*) at intermediate levels to salt marsh grass (*Puccinellia maritima*), sea pink (*Armeria maritima*) and sea lavender (*Limonium vulgare*) on the higher levels. The development of salt marshes clearly takes place over time as accretion raises the height of the marsh to allow other plants to colonise, yet it also develops over space and commonly encroaches across the tidal flat.

Salt marsh forms   The outward growth of salt marsh may be limited by the extent of shelter provided by an island or spit. These closed salt marshes do not display the clear zonation shown by the open salt marshes that occur within estuaries where development continues until it begins to encroach upon the central channel. Shifts in the central

Fig. 6.5 Erosion of the edge of a salt marsh caused by shifts in the central channel. Shannon Estuary, Co. Limerick, Ireland.

channel cause the oscillation of the outer edge of the marshland as it advances under depositional conditions and recedes during erosional scour (Fig. 6.5). Some creeks are abandoned in time as others become deeper and more efficient in carrying tidal flood and ebb. Abandonment allows infilling and colonisation of the creeks except where salt water collects and evaporates. The high salinity levels of these areas prevent vegetation colonisation and salt pans are the result. Pans produced by creek abandonment tend to be long and linear; circular pans may develop from unvegetated pools inherited from the original colonisation pattern.

On many European salt marshes, exceptionally large numbers of linear salt pans occur which suggests a recent change in conditions. Similarly, many salt marshes have small erosional cliffs or 'micro-falaise' on their seaward edges that are often difficult to explain solely in terms of shifts in the main channel. Small changes in sea-level are capable of producing both of these responses in the salt marsh environment and it will be seen later that global sea-levels have indeed varied in the recent past.

Mangrove swamp

In tropical regions and in many estuaries in Australia and South Africa, mangrove trees form the pioneer community that occupies the tidal flats. These tidal forests spread from the shores to colonise exposed mudflats, their extensive root systems slowing the tidal flow and encouraging deposition of fine sediment in the same way that the salt marsh vegetation of higher latitudes does. Mangroves are similarly drained by intricate creek systems which extend into the unvegetated mudflat. Mangrove encroachment onto tidal mudflats is indicated by an abundance of seedlings and young trees (see Fig. 2.13). The increase in size, age and coverage inland shows a broad species zonation similar to that found on a mid-latitude salt marsh. For example, in Florida mangrove communities the pioneer species, red mangrove (*Rhizophora mangle*), is replaced inland and higher up by black mangrove (*Avicennia germinans*) which mingles at its upper limit with a terrestrial forest of buttonwood and magnolia.

7   The influence of sea-level change

Each of the coastal landforms discussed so far has been examined in terms of the present-day processes of waves, sediment supply and tides. However, the equilibrium achieved between landform and process can occur only at present sea-level. It is, after all, the sea-level that determines *where* the coast occurs and therefore the precise location of beaches and to a lesser extent sand dunes. Imagine what the coastline of Britain would look like if the sea-level were to fall by 100 m! Yet that is approximately where the sea-level was a mere (geologically speaking) 18,000 years ago at the end of the Pleistocene period (Fig. 7.1). The coastal features that formed at this sea-level have been submerged by a subsequent rise but in other areas the land has been rising too, often outpacing the rise in sea-level. Coastal features are then left high and dry as *raised* or *fossil* shorelines (Fig. 7.2). Where these shifts in sea-level are rapid the old coastline lies abandoned at altitude (or depth), but where the shift is gradual, as with the present global sea-level rise of 0.2 cm/year, the landform may slowly adjust and migrate landwards.

The two types of sea-level change, global change and local change, must first be outlined before the coastal response can be examined.

Global sea-level change

Changes in global or *eustatic* sea-levels are principally the result of the wax and wane of large ice sheets which once covered much of the mid and high latitudes. As the glacial period began, water was held on land as ice rather than returned to the ocean in streams. Minor additions to global sea-level are thought to occur from the thermal expansion of ocean water during warm periods. However, *glacio-eustasy* is by far the major control, accounting for sea-level falls of between 100 m and 150 m during the Pleistocene period. In the last million years of the Pleistocene, nine complete glacial cycles are thought to have occurred; most is known about the last glacial period which culminated 18,000 years ago and its subsequent interglacial period, the Holocene, which commenced about 10,000 years ago. As far as sea-level is concerned, the development of a glacial period results in a slow sea-level fall or *regression*, leading to the emergence of large areas of former sea floor. Interglacials are characterised by rapid *transgression* or sea-level rise which floods the land. Because of the broad similarity in the amount of sea-level rise and fall in each cycle, many coastal features may have been reoccupied by subsequent sea-levels, but it is the last regression/transgression cycle that has had most influence on the form of our present coastal features. In the last 18,000 years most coasts have been submerged, or more accurately re-submerged, by sea-level rise (Fig. 7.1).

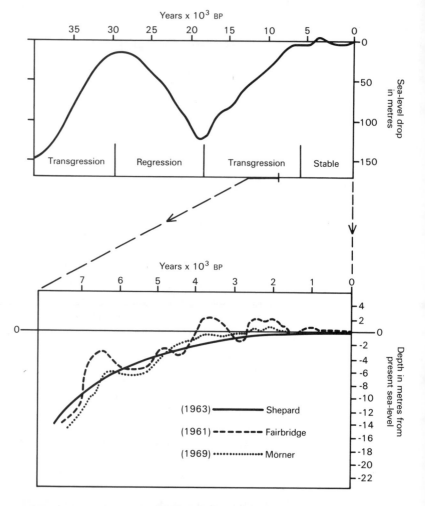

Fig. 7.1 Sea-level fluctuations in the last 35,000 years before present (BP). The curve in the upper diagram is based on only limited data whereas the lower curves show that considerable disagreement exists over the position of sea-levels during the last 7,000 years or so. Increasingly it is recognised that single global sea-level curves like these may be unrealistic in view of the likelihood of local and regional tectonic coastal changes affecting sea-level position. Source: modified from Komar (1976).

Fig. 7.2 Raised pebble beach at 25–30 m above sea-level in Glenbatrick, Isle of Jura, Strathclyde. The house is built on a lower and younger raised beach that is also composed of pebbles.

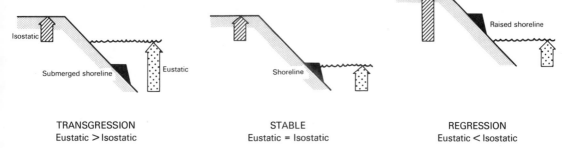

TRANSGRESSION
Eustatic > Isostatic

STABLE
Eustatic = Isostatic

REGRESSION
Eustatic < Isostatic

Fig. 7.3 Mechanisms of shoreline elevation. Where eustatic sea-level rise exceeds isostatic (or tectonic) land rise, the shoreline becomes submerged; where land rise exceeds sea-level rise, raised shorelines occur.

Local sea-level change

Superimposed on the eustatic change in sea-level are local changes caused principally by tectonic uplift and isostasy. In *tectonically* active areas, emerged marine terraces indicate that the level of the land may be rising faster than eustatic rise, for example in Japan, New Zealand and in parts of the Mediterranean basin. This slow process is spectacularly accelerated during earthquakes when the shoreline is elevated virtually instantaneously. For example, the shoreline displacement caused by the Chilean earthquake of 1835 was recorded graphically by Charles Darwin on board HMS *Beagle:*

> 'Captain Fitzroy found beds of putrid mussel-shells adhering to the rocks ten feet above the high-water . . . the inhabitants [of the island of Santa Maria] had formerly dived at low-water springs for these shells . . .'

Local sea-level changes occur outside the tectonically active areas and the most important of these results from *glacio-isostasy*. During glacial periods water loads are transferred from the oceans to the much smaller glaciated areas. On deglaciation the depression of the land surface caused by the weight of ice ceases and uplift commences. The rate of uplift is slow at first, followed by a rapid uplift phase which again slows as uplift nears completion. Thus beaches and coastal features formed when the land was more depressed become elevated, like the raised beaches and terraces of Scotland. There are two important modifications to this general picture of coastal uplift. Figure 7.1 shows that the rate of eustatic sea-level change also varied; for example, it rose fairly quickly between 18,000 and 6,000 years ago and then levelled off. For beaches to become elevated the isostatic rise of the land must exceed the eustatic rise of the sea (Fig. 7.3). In much of Scotland at present, isostatic uplift still outpaces eustatic rise and regression continues, giving rise to suites of raised beaches (see Fig. 7.2). The second modification to the uplift pattern is a spatial one. The amount of uplift depends on the thickness and weight of ice originally covering the area. The British ice was at its thickest in western central Scotland where subsequently maximum uplift occurred, with a progressive decline in all directions away from this area. Shorelines of the same age therefore became elevated by different amounts depending on the distance from the ice centre. For example, a walk along the raised rock shoreline on the islands of Scarba, Jura and Islay in the Inner Hebrides will confirm a shoreline tilt towards the uplift centre (Fig. 7.4). Elsewhere isostatic uplift was weak and was overtaken by an eustatic rise in sea-level which flooded the coast during the Holocene

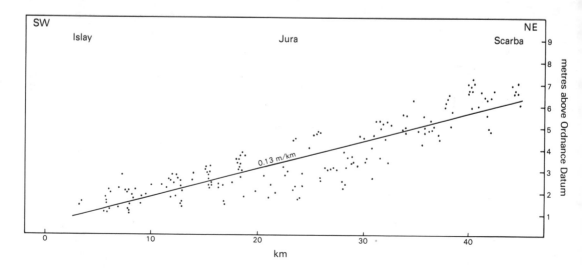

Fig. 7.4 A tilted rock shoreline caused by differential isostatic uplift in the Inner Hebrides, Strathclyde. The centre of isostatic uplift lies to the north-east. Source: after Dawson (1980).

interglacial period. The present weak uplift pattern of submergence in the north and west of Scotland, Wales and England and emergence in central Scotland reflects this.

Coastal response to sea-level change

It is clear from the above account that the effects of global sea-level change vary from place to place depending on local tectonic or isostatic change. The net result of these interactions is a *relative sea-level* that may vary from positive to negative in the lifetime of any coastal landform. Coastal response to sea-level change is also conditioned by the angle of the coastal slope and by the volume of sediment available for deposition.

Coastal slope

For any given sea-level change, the horizontal movement of the shoreline is faster where low-gradient coastal slopes occur (Fig. 7.5a). For example, the horizontal extension of the southern North Sea during the early Holocene period is known to have been very rapid because of low gradients and rates of shoreline migration of 60–70 m/year were not uncommon (Fig. 7.5b). This rapid rise in sea-level and migration of the shoreline had important consequences for the spread of species colonising the British Isles as the climate improved. The *land bridges* which connected Europe, Britain and Ireland were rapidly inundated and formed barriers to northward and westward-moving colonisers (Fig. 7.5b). Species such as the shrew and the badger did not cross the land bridge to Ireland before it was flooded (Table 7.1). Snakes also failed to make the crossing (although the lack of Irish snakes is commonly credited to the activities of St Patrick!).

Sediment availability

Coastal response to changes in sea-level is also determined by the amount and availability of sediment both from offshore and from rivers. During the low sea-levels of the Pleistocene period, large amounts of glacier-derived materials were deposited on the continental shelf. The

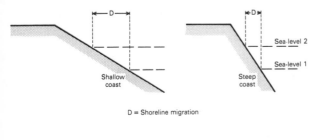

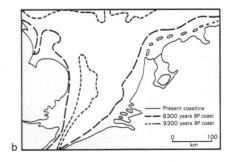

a

b

rapidly rising Holocene sea-level swept up much of this sediment into beaches. When the rapid rise ended about 6,000 years ago (Fig. 7.1), conditions were suitable for beach development to reach a maximum and for windblown sand to build large sand dune complexes. However, in the stable or slowly rising sea-level since, little new sediment has been brought within wave action and the amount of material supplied from offshore has slowly become exhausted. Beaches have begun to erode.

Table 7.1 The floras and faunas of Britain and Ireland compared.

Species	Britain	Ireland
Plants	1,349	907
Land mammals	32	14
Birds	456	354
Reptiles	4	1
Amphibians	6	2

Source: Mitchell (1976).

This sequence may be locally reversed by high inputs of fluvial sediment. In Britain and the mid latitudes, large loads of fluvial sediment were delivered to the coast during deglaciation but the present-day amounts are limited mainly to the river exits themselves. In currently glaciated areas and in low latitudes the quantities of fluvial sediment delivered still reach proportions large enough to offset the effect of Holocene sea-level rise.

Modelling coastal response

Over the last 18,000 years, *relative* sea-levels have continuously varied depending on location. Similarly, the delivery of sediment from both fluvial and offshore sources has also varied. The coastal response to both groups of variables can be seen in Fig. 7.6 where positive and negative relative sea-level changes are matched against erosion and deposition. Three main types of coastal response emerge from Fig. 7.6:

1 *Transgression*   During most of the Holocene period, rapid sea-level rise has outstripped the rate of sediment deposition, leading to the landward migration of the shoreline. Much of the south and east of England falls into this category, with the transgression flooding areas of once dry land. There are numerous examples of submerged forest and peat beds at or below sea-level in southern Britain. The submerged forest at Borth, Dyfed is interesting (see Fig. 4.7) for it provides evidence of the rapid Holocene submergence of the

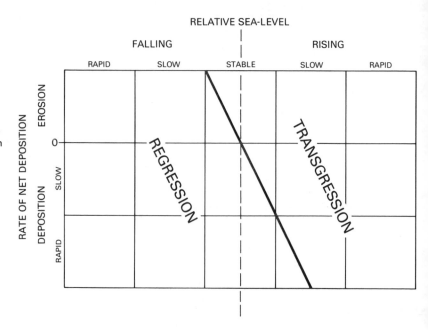

Fig. 7.6 Regression and transgression of shorelines occurs as sea-level rises and falls and as the rates of net sediment deposition varies. A slow sea-level rise, that might otherwise result in a transgression landwards, can be offset by a high rate of deposition that allows the coastline to build seawards as a regression. This often occurs at river mouths. An adjacent coast with a lower rate of coastal deposition may suffer coastal retreat as a result of the same sea-level rise. Source: Curray (1964).

low-gradient floor of Cardigan Bay. Students of Welsh folklore already know of this flooding from the legend of Cantref-y-Gwaelod, the lost land of Cardigan Bay. It is possible that the Neolithic peoples who are known to have occupied the area may have witnessed enough of the submergence to commit it to memory and legend. It is also likely that many British beaches formed during this transgression have moved onshore by a 'rolling-over' process, keeping pace with the sea-level rise by transgressing shorewards. The process continues today at beaches such as Chesil Beach in Dorset (Fig. 4.6), Slapton Sands in Devon and on the magnificent barrier coast at Ballyteige, Tacumshin and Lady's Island in Co. Wexford, Ireland.

2   *Static*   This situation occurs where the rising relative sea-level is balanced by a sedimentation rate that allows the shoreline to keep pace vertically with sea-level rise even when the landward area becomes flooded to create a lagoon. There is continual reworking of sediments, giving rise to shoreface cut-and-fill sequences (Chapter 4) built on top of one another. The barrier islands of the eastern USA and Gulf coasts are perhaps the best examples of this, although many are now beginning to narrow or migrate shorewards as sea-level rises and sediment supplies diminish.

3   *Regression*   Where the supply of sediment is locally abundant or where relative sea-level has fallen, as in the isostatically uplifted areas of Britain, the coast moves seawards. The volume of sediment from the great deltas of the world or from updrift erosion as in the Dungeness foreland in Kent (Fig. 4.14), have reversed the Holocene transgression to allow building out from the coast. The coast builds out by the addition of beach ridges on the seaward face and a wide coastal plain or foreland is the result. Many such features first began to develop some time after 6000 BP when the rate of sea-level rise slackened and allowed deposition to dominate in suitable areas. In Britain, with the notable exception of Dungeness, much of this regression was – and still is – confined to areas of uplift or to

estuaries and inlets. In regions where sediment input is still high, regression of the outer coast continues. In Iceland the supply of large quantities of fluvio-glacial sediment has resulted in spectacular regression of the storm-dominated south coast; the coast of Myrdalssandur moved seawards during a flood in 1918 by 200 m!

It should be noted that over the period of development of any one coastal landform, all three types of response may occur. For example, at Newborough Warren in Anglesey the area was transgressed during the Holocene as the relative sea-level rose quickly. This was probably followed by a brief static period and then by regression after 6000 BP when large volumes of sediment were delivered to the coast, the excess sediment being blown into the sand dunes which now mask the original beach ridges. Today, due to a reduction in sediment supply and a slight relative sea-level rise, a slow transgression has replaced regression and there is erosion of the beach and sand dunes. For similar reasons, the erosion at Newborough is matched by erosion of beaches in much of Europe, North America, Australia and New Zealand, amongst other places.

Present global sea-level rise

The overriding reason for coastal recession in many parts of the world may relate to the present 0.1–0.3 cm/year increase in eustatic sea-level. This rise in sea-level, recorded by tide-gauges from London Bridge to

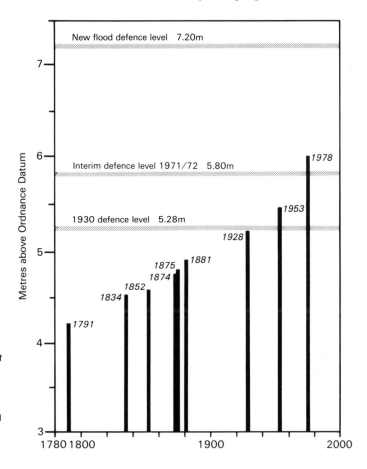

Fig. 7.7 High tide and storm surge heights at London Bridge have increased by about 1 m in the last hundred years. In view of this, the new flood defence level provided by the Thames Barrier is designed to be substantially higher than the 1930 and 1971 defence levels. Source: modified from Goudie (1983).

75

Honolulu, is due to a general amelioration of climate which has caused the retreat of glaciers in many parts of the world over the last 100 years. In addition to the contribution made by glacial meltwater, the increase in global air temperatures has led to a slight warming of ocean waters and a resulting small rise in sea-level. On many coasts, this sea-level rise has resulted in slow migration of the shoreline and beach landwards. In some localities, land subsidence has combined with eustatic sea-level rise to threaten low-lying coastal land with inundation. Historical tide-gauge records for London Bridge show high-tide and storm-surge levels to have increased by 1 m between 1852 and 1953 (Fig. 7.7). The increase in ordinary high-tide levels is somewhat lower but the risk of major flood damage to central London resulted in the construction of the Thames Barrier in 1983. Similar tidal barriers have been built at Barking on the Thames in Greater London, at Hull on the River Hull in Humberside and are planned for the Italian city of Venice. However, this view of global sea-level rise is not universally accepted since tide-gauges themselves may be subject to local tectonic activity that must be decoded from global sea-level effects.

8   People and coasts

Until very recently the coastal zone was only thinly occupied by those whose livelihoods were concerned with the sea. Small fishing and trading ports situated in sheltered locations were the norm and the rest of the coast was either in agricultural use or in its natural state. Settlements originally sited in locations subject to flooding, erosion or sand inundation were often short-lived or abandoned. For example, a large part of the medieval town of Dunwich in Suffolk was destroyed in a storm and thereafter it declined in importance. However, over the last 200 years or so, the amount of coastal development has rapidly increased with port expansion and industrialisation and with extensive spread of settlement along the coastal zone (Fig. 8.1). Inevitably, this expansion further along the coast has led to problems of erosion, for in spite of the essentially dynamic and flexible nature of the coast, humans want constructions to be static and regard their boundary lines as inflexible. In the heyday of engineering during the nineteenth and early twentieth centuries the solutions to erosion problems on the British coast inevitably involved construction of the seawalls, groynes, breakwaters and piers that are with us today.

It is important to note that however obvious the problems of *coastal erosion* are, they are only one part of a range of physical pressures now facing the coastal zone. Along with the increase in consumption of coastal land has been an increase in the use of coastal waters for transporting fuel and goods and for dumping unwanted wastes. The consequent problems of accidental and deliberate pollution of coastal waters poses a great threat to the use of the coastal sea as both a fishing and recreational resource. In view of such diverse pressures, there is an increasing need for *coastal management* to help safeguard the coast for the future.

Coastal erosion in history

Coastal erosion is an emotive term: it threatens. Yet it is worth remembering that the hazard of coastal erosion is only recognised as such where people are involved and where life, building land and livestock are in danger. On deserted shores, the recession of the coast is seen as a natural process that may be reversed at some (unspecified) time in the future. It is perhaps this unspecified time element that we have been most ignorant, or intolerant, of in the past. Many erosion problems have arisen simply because of deliberate interference with coastal processes themselves. Other problems occur where development has taken place on low-lying or submerging coasts where coastal flooding may accompany erosion, as in the Netherlands and Lincolnshire. Relatively high coasts may be subject to long-term erosion also; the 15–20 m-high glacial till cliffs of Norfolk are retreating at

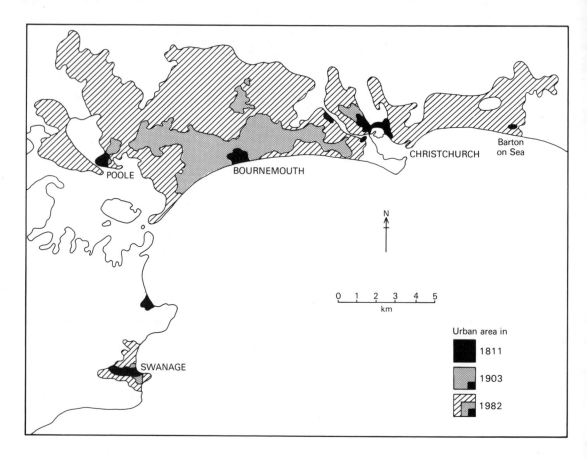

Urban area in
■ 1811
▨ 1903
▨ 1982

Fig. 8.1 Urbanisation of the coastal zone in the Bournemouth area, Dorset. Over the last few centuries expansion similar to that shown has occurred in almost all coastal towns in the British Isles. For example, Blackpool in Lancashire increased its developed coastal frontage from 1.2 km in 1850 to 13.3 km by 1965, a more than tenfold increase! (See Clayton, 1979.)

1–2 m/year and the chalk cliffs at Dieppe in northern France recede at 0.4 m/year. Early maps, historical documents and now photographs provide an invaluable source of information about coastal change. The 57 km-long coastline of Holderness in Humberside has been particularly well documented as far back as the Domesday Survey in AD 1086. Even in the Icelandic literature, Hrafnseyrr or 'Hrafn's sandbank', later to become Ravenser Spurn and then Spurn Point, at the southern tip of Holderness, was regularly referred to before 1066. Since the Domesday Survey almost 30 small towns and villages along this part of the coast have disappeared into the sea, along with the cliffs on which they stood (Fig. 8.2). Since Roman times the coastline has retreated by over 4 km. The Meaux Chronicle records the gruesome result of the erosion of the coastal town of Ravenser Odd between 1350 and 1355. When the chapel of St Mary was destroyed, the graveyard was washed away so that bodies 'horribly appeared' and had to be reburied. Some time after 1362 the town was eventually destroyed and the submerged remains of the road and buildings caused frequent shipwrecks. The erosion continues today, the most recent casualties being a row of holiday homes at Skipsea which were destroyed in 1984 (Fig. 8.3).

Medieval Dunwich in Suffolk suffered a similar fate. Records show that in 1222, King Henry III granted £200 towards the cost of sea defences and later, in the fourteenth and fifteenth centuries, the four churches of St Michael, St Leonard, St Martin and St John the Baptist all either collapsed into the sea or were pulled down. Erosion had therefore already been severe prior to a detailed survey in 1589 which showed a sizeable town still in existence. Between 1589 and 1753, when

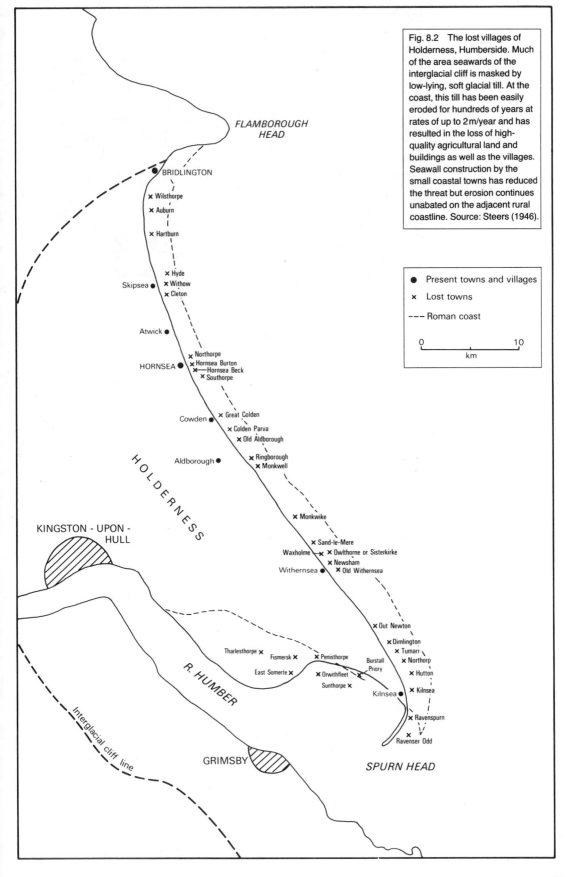

Fig. 8.2 The lost villages of Holderness, Humberside. Much of the area seawards of the interglacial cliff is masked by low-lying, soft glacial till. At the coast, this till has been easily eroded for hundreds of years at rates of up to 2 m/year and has resulted in the loss of high-quality agricultural land and buildings as well as the villages. Seawall construction by the small coastal towns has reduced the threat but erosion continues unabated on the adjacent rural coastline. Source: Steers (1946).

● Present towns and villages
× Lost towns
--- Roman coast

0   10
        km

FLAMBOROUGH HEAD

● BRIDLINGTON
× Wilsthorpe
× Auburn
× Hartburn

× Hyde
Skipsea ●   × Withow
× Cleton

Atwick ●

× Northorpe
× Hornsea Burton
HORNSEA ●   — Hornsea Beck
× Southorpe

Cowden ●   × Great Colden
× Colden Parva
× Old Aldborough

Aldborough ●   × Ringborough
× Monkwell

H O L D E R N E S S

× Monkwike

× Sand-le-Mere
Waxholme   × Owlthorne or Sisterkirke
× Newsham
Withernsea ●   × Old Withernsea

KINGSTON - UPON - HULL

× Out Newton

× Dimlington
× Tumarr
Tharlesthorpe ×   × Northorp
Fismersk ×   × Penisthorpe   Burstall Priory   × Hutton
East Somerte ×   × Orwithfleet
Sunthorpe ×   × Kilnsea
Kilnsea ●
R. HUMBER
Interglacial cliff line
× Ravenspurn
×
Ravenser Odd

GRIMSBY   SPURN HEAD

79

Fig. 8.3 Lost houses at Skipsea, Holderness. In the few years before 1980 (when the photograph was taken) these holiday houses had become increasingly threatened by erosion of the till cliff on which they stood. By 1984, they had become unsafe and were removed. In the next decade, much of the site area of the houses will have been eroded and the old access road to the rear will be under threat.

the coast was mapped again, a large part of Dunwich was eroded at a rate of 1.54 m/year. Erosion has declined in recent years, probably because of the extension of an offshore sheltering sandbank.

Much of old Brighton in East Sussex was lost to the sea between 1292 and 1705. The remaining town was eroding at such an alarming rate in 1723 that £1,700 was raised to construct two groynes to halt the recession. It now seems likely that only Brighton's rapid transformation from a poor fishing town to a favoured health resort prevented it from being left to fall into the sea. Ongoing erosion of the adjacent coastline continued and only 10 now remain of the 47 Martello towers built on the Sussex coast during the Napoleonic wars to warn England of invasion.

Present-day coastal erosion

It is becoming increasingly clear that erosion prevails on many of the world's coasts. For example, the coastline of Europe suffers widespread erosion (Fig. 8.4), although regression is more common in the isostatically uplifted areas of Scotland and Fennoscandia, the tectonically uplifted parts of the Mediterranean and where fluvial sediment supply is still high. In the British Isles, in spite of an apparent predominance of erosion, more land has been gained than lost since about 1870. The Royal Commission on Coast Erosion and Afforestation reported in 1911 that gains of land exceeded losses but that the foreshore was steepening, indicating a net loss of sediment volume on the coast (Table 8.1). All of the gains had been made by deposition and reclamation *in the estuaries*, however, and the erosional losses were borne by the *outer coast*. This pattern is essentially maintained today with ongoing and widespread erosion of the outer coast. In the east and south of England defence works now proliferate to the extent that 55 per cent of the coastline of Kent, Sussex and Hampshire is protected from erosion by seawalls.

It is now widely acknowledged that the best defence against coastal

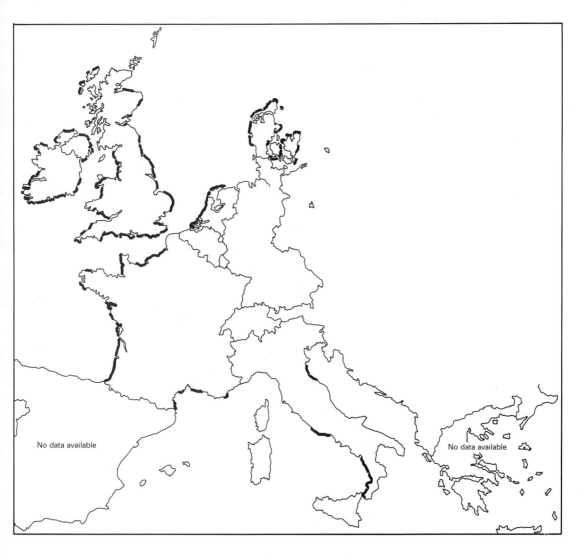

No data available

No data available

Fig. 8.4 Sites of coastal erosion in the EEC. Coastal erosion is a widespread problem in Europe. Soft coastal rocks, open exposure and strong longshore currents promote erosion but the problems are often exacerbated by human interference such as quarrying of beaches for sand and gravel, removal of protective vegetation cover and poorly designed seawalls. Source: Commission of European Communities (1987).

erosion is a wide beach capable of absorbing all of the energy of waves as they move up the shore. Erosion occurs when sufficient wave energy remains at the top of the beach, or base of the cliff, to remove material. The general conditions under which beaches are cut under storm waves, and cliffs and shore platforms eroded under breaking waves, were outlined in Chapters 2 and 3. However, it is necessary here to sketch the background conditions against which such erosion takes place. The

Table 8.1 Areas gained and lost over a period averaging 35 years prior to 1904.

	Land area (hectares)		Foreshore area (hectares)	
	Gain	Loss	Gain	Loss
England and Wales	14,344	1,899	5,422	18,061
Scotland	1,904	330	1,650	5,037
Ireland	3,178	458	2,250	5,274
Total	19,426	2,687	9,322	28,372

Source: H.M.S.O. (1911).

influence of those background factors varies from place to place but the main ones are discussed below in approximate order of importance.

Global sea-level rise

Eustatic sea-level rise is regarded by many as being at the very heart of erosion and flooding problems today. Slow sea-level rise results in landward migration of the shoreline and increasing degrees of wave attack on land once beyond wave reach. On the low-lying shores of the North Sea, the area prone to erosion and subsequent flooding greatly increases as sea-level rises. Invariably, it is during temporary elevation of the sea-surface during storm surges that the ongoing sea-level rise is first manifest. Storm surge elevations have increased through time owing to global sea-level rise (see Fig. 7.7). In some areas, notably in the USA, there is evidence that the frequency of severe storms has increased and that this is responsible for accelerated beach erosion. As yet there appears to be limited evidence of this increase in Europe but as global sea-level increases, so too will the frequency of storms *above* a given height.

On high coasts the adjustment of the coastal profile to wave conditions takes longer than on low-lying and depositional coasts and many of these high coasts have not yet fully adjusted their morphology to present processes. On the rapidly eroding high coasts composed of glacial till and clay, unabated cliff retreat over time (since Roman times in eastern England) suggests that lowering of the offshore till surface is continuing to keep pace with cliff retreat (see Fig. 8.3). Reduction of erosion rates and adjustment of landforms is even more unlikely if sea-levels continue to rise.

Reduction in sediment supply

The decline in the previously plentiful offshore sediment source is thought to be partly responsible for global erosion (see Chapter 7). In addition to the reduction in offshore sediment from its peak availability shortly after 6000 BP, there is evidence to indicate that there has been a more recent decline in fluvial supply. This sediment supply declined in the Holocene period owing to expanded vegetation cover and has been further reduced by human activity. Severe erosion of up to 40m/year of the once-advancing Nile delta in Egypt is probably related to the interception of river sediments by barrages and dams upstream. The sediment yield of the Rhône in France has plummeted from 40 million tonnes/year in the 1900s to 4–5 million tonnes/year in 1970, owing to dam construction. Coastal erosion of the Rhône delta has ensued and Stes Maries-de-la-Mer, once an inland town, is now protected by breakwaters. Due to the relatively unimportant contribution of rivers to most of the British coast, the reduction in sediment supply here is mainly related to declining offshore sources.

Interference with natural coastal processes

The coincidence of severe erosion and areas of concentrated coastal development is striking and principally related to the building of structures in the coastal zone designed to improve navigation or to

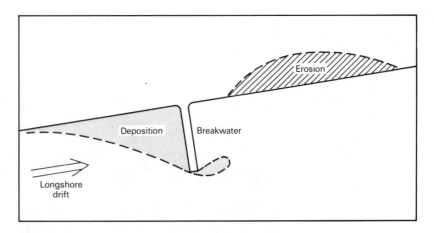

Fig. 8.5 The erosion that occurs downdrift of breakwaters and groynes is the result of the damming of sediment on the updrift side of the structure (see also Fig. 4.9).

diminish coastal erosion. Another cause of erosion is the deliberate removal of beach dune and offshore sediment for building purposes.

1 *Jetties and breakwaters* Beaches are supplied with sediments from offshore and alongshore and so the interruption of either source reduces beach volumes. Jetties are built at river mouths or inlets to stabilise the channel or to prevent shoaling. They often project beyond the breaker zone and so act as a partial or total block to longshore drift with the result that sediment accumulation on the updrift side causes shoreline advance, whereas reduced sediment supply on the downdrift side causes shoreline retreat (Fig. 8.5). Breakwaters are built to provide a harbour that is sheltered from waves and in the same way as jetties, they may either interrupt longshore drift or diminish the wave energy at the shore, thereby causing deposition. In either case, breakwaters reduce the capacity of waves to move material alongshore and so enhance erosion downdrift. At Newhaven in East Sussex, a breakwater built to protect the harbour entrance greatly reduced the longshore drift that formerly supplied sediments to the Seaford beaches to the east. Seaford built seawalls and groynes to combat this erosion but erosion of the chalk cliffs of Seaford Head to the east was accelerated. Similarly the piers built at Gorleston in Norfolk acted as a dam to the southward drift of sediment, starving the areas of Corton and Lowestoft and causing erosion of the sand and gravel cliffs. Lowestoft subsequently built a seawall to protect against this erosion. In the USA, erosion of beaches up to 20 km downcoast followed breakwater construction at Santa Barbara, California. At nearby Santa Monica, an entire city block was eroded away after a similar structure was built. At both, sand by-pass schemes now continuously suck impounded sand and pump it onto downdrift beaches. At similar places worldwide, longshore drift now depends on human help!

On coasts where there is no net longshore drift, jetties and breakwaters have been successful, yet it is apparent that their construction on coasts where longshore drift is important may cause the export of erosion downdrift. Groynes have a similar effect in that these intertidal walls are designed to trap longshore-moving sediment and locally enhance beach volumes, thus reducing the amount of sediment exported downdrift (see Fig. 4.9). The coastline downdrift of the groynes at Hornsea in Humberside suffers

Fig. 8.6 Downdrift erosion at Hornsea, Humberside is accelerated by the trapping of sediment in the seawall and groyne system in front of the town. The beach downdrift is thus starved of sediment that would otherwise maintain the beach and help reduce the rate of erosion.

Fig. 8.7 The near-vertical seawall at Aberystwyth, Dyfed has caused extensive beach lowering due to wave reflection and scour. The beach is now artificially maintained in order to reduce the threat of undermining.

accelerated erosion because of reduced sediment supply to the cliff-foot beach (Fig. 8.6).

2 *Seawalls, bulkheads and revetments*   These are intended to prevent wave erosion of the landward area and so are built parallel to the shoreline, generally out of materials such as concrete or natural stone. Many of the older seawalls were built vertically as this form is a relatively cheap and efficient reflector of waves. However, since the wave energy is reflected, increased scour results in removal of sediments, erosion of the toe and possible failure of the wall itself.

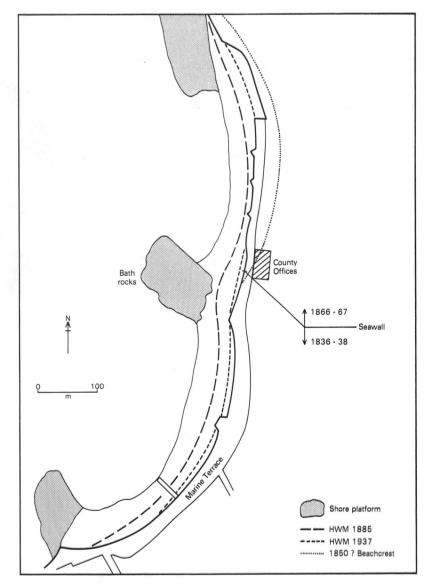

Fig. 8.8 Construction of the northern seawall at Aberystwyth in 1866 was well seaward of the natural line of the original beach. Problems still dog the seawall (see Fig. 8.7). Source: Wood (1978).

Bath rocks

County Offices

↑ 1866 - 67
———— Seawall
↓ 1836 - 38

N

0   100
      m

Marine Terrace

Shore platform

— — HWM 1885
- - - - HWM 1937
·········· 1850 ? Beachcrest

Destruction of the seawalls by such undermining resulted in enforced realignment inland of the Dublin to Wexford railway between Killiney in Co. Dublin and Greystones in Co. Wicklow, Ireland. The construction of a seawall in Aberystwyth, Dyfed in 1866 created wave reflection and toe erosion that is still a problem today (Fig. 8.7). The wall was built in a straight line across the beach whose crest had originally extended in a wide crescent landwards of the wall's present position (Fig. 8.8). Erosion gradually reduced beach levels so that by 1937 the seawall suffered a major collapse through undermining and a massive replacement seawall was built slightly seaward. This did nothing to improve conditions and the beach is now artificially maintained with pebbles brought in from elsewhere. Seawalls now tend to be constructed with a shallow slope to diminish reflection. They are also constructed of roughly surfaced or loosely packed blocks or gabions (Fig. 8.9) to enhance permeability and so reduce the reflection problems which have dogged many traditional seawalls.

Fig. 8.9 Wherever possible, modern seawall constructions should present low-angled semi-permeable or rough surfaces. In this example, boulder-filled cages or gabions have been set at a low angle and this has enabled a healthy beach to develop and blown sand from the beach to accumulate on the gabions. Colonisation by marram grass helps camouflage the structure. Aberdeen Bay, Grampian.

In addition to reflection and scour, two other problems affect all seawalls. The first is that their very purpose is to prevent erosion of the land behind. Such erosion formerly provided sediments for the beach in front and, via longshore drift, for nourishment of downdrift beaches. Sterilisation of these *feeder bluffs* by seawall construction may therefore create erosion downdrift. Second, when seawalls are built on an eroding shoreline (a common location), the adjacent and unprotected shoreline continues to erode, for example at Withernsea in Humberside and at Cromer in Norfolk. This creates flank erosion and the seawall may be weakened from the sides at first and then from behind. To combat the erosion of adjacent coastal sections, the seawall may be extended laterally to become virtually self-propagating. The coastal defences of Blackpool in Lancashire largely developed in this fashion. The logical conclusion seems to be that partial protection of an eroding coast will lead to future problems. It may be more satisfactory either to protect the whole eroding area or not to protect it at all; either strategy has its pitfalls.

3   *Sand and gravel extraction*   Most coastal sediment extraction is for construction purposes, and it can have damaging effects on the coast. Offshore gravel extraction alters sea-floor geometry, allowing bigger waves to reach the shore, and this may affect longshore drift. Little is known of the relationship between offshore banks and shoreline equilibrium, particularly with respect to sediment exchange, although in East Anglia the location of erosion and deposition zones on the coast is thought to be controlled by the position of offshore banks, as at Dunwich. In view of this, the continued extraction of shallow-depth marine gravels in the south and east of the North Sea does not appear particularly farsighted, especially as these areas are also where shoreline erosion is widespread. Extraction from the beach itself is reckless, as a wide beach is a good coastal protector. The village of Hallsands in Devon was protected by a large shingle ridge before seabed and intertidal dredging removed 650,000 tonnes of it between 1897 and 1901.

During the storms of 1903 and 1917, the much-reduced ridge was removed and the village destroyed; in one night, 27 houses were washed into the sea. The lesson of Hallsands has not been learned. Erosion and flooding, requiring substantial expenditure to alleviate, continued at Chesil Beach in Dorset (Fig. 4.6) for many years. In spite of this, extraction of the beach material only ceased in 1986 as a result of a public inquiry. Foreshore erosion at Portobello beach in Scotland, following the removal of sand for a local glassworks, lowered the beach by 2 m. Ironically, this popular recreational beach was restored by replacing the beach with sand 'borrowed' from the floor of the Firth of Forth. Removal of sand from British beaches is now illegal except under licence, yet in many remote areas of Scotland and in the western and northern isles, sand is still regularly removed, often from eroding beaches.

Responses to coastal erosion

There are three main ways in which erosion may be tackled: structural response, non-structural response, and 'do nothing' response.

Structural response

Traditionally, coastal engineers have concentrated on fixing the coastline in space and have employed the structures mentioned above in their struggle against the sea. In many situations such a response has been successful but in others there has been accelerated erosion. A frequent problem is the self-propagating nature of structures where down-coast locations are starved of sediment and are then forced to protect themselves. One novel approach is simply to move the shoreline seawards by the building of a series of offshore islands, allowing the shoreline to stabilise in between. This has been successfully attempted in the Great Lakes of North America. However, the application of such schemes on an exposed eroding coast such as the English east coast is more questionable. Developments over the years have included the design of shallow-angled and permeable seawalls designed to mimic beach processes. This takes the coastal engineer closest to the ideal solution: that of replacing the beach itself.

Non-structural response

Beach nourishment strategies have now been employed for many years on beaches worldwide. For example, Waikiki Beach in Hawaii is periodically trucked in from 14 km away. Copacabana Beach in Rio de Janeiro, Brazil was rebuilt in 1970 with sand from a nearby bay. Careful matching of the 'borrow' material to the natural beach sediment is required for nourishment to be successful in reducing erosion yet retaining the character of the beach. This is important where the beach is a local recreational asset. Beach nourishment allows the beach to function normally and as this includes longshore drift, downdrift beaches suffer no erosion as a result of the strategy since their sediment supply is maintained. However, periodic refilling of the beach is necessary, although at, say, 10-year intervals, this may be more economical than protecting by seawall and groyne (see Fig. 1.1). Since 1974, beaches in Bournemouth, Dorset have been extended as a result of beach nourishment using sand from banks several kilometres offshore. In East Sussex, the beach between Camber and Pett is regularly recharged with pebbles.

Another non-structural response is to stabilise the eroding area by reducing its slope, draining, and planting with vegetation. Many coastal cliffs, particularly those in clay or glacial till, are subject to slumping during wet conditions. The waves at their base often simply remove the slumped and weakened material. By regrading these slopes using bulldozers and by providing efficient drainage, the stability of such coastal cliffs is enhanced. Planted with shrubs, trees and short grasses and with minimal toe protection in the form of a low wall or wooden bulkhead, a previously unsightly eroding cliff may be transformed into a recreational asset. Inevitably, during stabilisation some cliff-top land may be forfeited in order to regrade the coastal slope. Successful cliff stabilisation schemes have been implemented, for example at Whitby in North Yorkshire and at Bournemouth in Dorset.

The strategies adopted in sand dune areas are slightly different, perhaps because, being largely undeveloped, some recession is tolerable. Frontal erosion of sand dunes is the most serious problem and responses here include bulldozing, brushwood fencing and marram planting. Bulldozing an eroded dune back into an aerodynamic shape has proved successful at the Portrush dunes in Ulster. A similar strategy was adopted to rehabilitate the dunes at St Fergus, Grampian where gas pipelines from offshore fields make their landfall. Following bulldozer operations, the bare sand slope was covered with netting, sprayed with a tar substance and then planted with marram dug from adjacent dunes. Brushwood fencing has also been successfully employed in dune building. Deposition eventually covers the fence and a new fence is constructed on top of the old one. The new dune is then planted with dune grasses. At Newborough Warren in Anglesey, two dune ridges were 'artificially inseminated' by this process in the early 1960s (Fig. 8.10).

Brushwood fencing and marram planting is also employed in stabilising blow-outs inland from the beach. In addition 'thatching', or the use of cuttings from trees (usually conifers) strewn on the dune surface, enhances deposition. Marram can then be planted or in some cases, conifers themselves may be planted. The great dune fields of Culbin on the Moray Firth (see Fig. 4.11) were stabilised in this manner and the mobile dunes which engulfed Culbin estate in 1694 now support a mature forest. Dunes are an important recreational resource and this has led to trampling problems at popular sites, particularly over the summer months. Destruction of vegetation and blow-out development has occurred at Ynyslas, Dyfed, for example, owing to pedestrian pressure, and at Achmelvich and Clachtoll, Highland region, as a result of vehicles and caravans. Management responses have involved restriction of access by fencing and paving dune pathways, rehabilitation of eroded surfaces by planting and brushwood fencing and the erection of information boards. Such boards are an important

Fig. 8.10 These artificial dunes at Newborough Warren, Anglesey were produced by brushwood fencing in order to stabilise the coast and help protect commercial forestry from wind and salt damage.

feature, as an informed public is more likely to be co-operative and to respect restrictions of access.

'Do nothing' response

At first glance this hardly seems an appropriate action (or inaction) to take, yet for centuries people who have lived with natural hazards like coastal erosion have rationalised this by accepting that little can be done in the face of such 'acts of God'. However, in the last century engineering solutions have been sought and in many cases found wanting. Increasingly the question that coastal residents facing erosion must ask themselves is not '*How* can we protect?' but first '*Should* we protect?'. In some cases, large capital expenditure on coast defences has been ill-advised and subsequent failure has led to an outcry as at Barton-on-Sea in Dorset in the early 1970s. The £1.3-million coastal defence scheme at Barton lay in ruins in 1975, four years after its completion. A long and bitter dispute ensued between local residents and the authorities over whether or not to protect and which methods to use if protection was decided on. The issue has never been fully resolved. In other areas the cost of any coast protection scheme is so high in comparison with the value of the land lost as to make it completely uneconomic, e.g. on the Holderness coast of Humberside and at Walton-on-the-Naze in Suffolk. In any case, protection of only part of the eroding shore may have knock-on effects downcoast. In 1984 it became government policy in Britain to view undeveloped sections of the coast as inappropriate for grant-aided protection. An urban area on this eroding coast is, however, eligible. The problems created by partial protection of eroding coasts spring from a reluctance to view the coast as an interdependent system where manipulation of one part forces a reaction in another. Management of the entire coast offers one way forward.

Coastal management

Pressures

In terms of coastal erosion problems there is a clear argument to treat the coast as a whole, irrespective of town and administrative

Fig. 8.11 Spoil from coal mining is tipped into the nearshore zone at Seaham, Tyne and Wear. Longshore transport of the spoil discolours the sea-water and moves coal waste for many kilometres downdrift, resulting in degraded beaches and a derelict coastline.

boundaries. Yet the coast is also under pressure from development and pollution. Industrial and urban expansion (see Fig. 8.1) creates pressure on coastal land. Flat sites near deep water are often sought for, amongst other developments, petrochemical complexes, container terminals and power stations, and sizeable stretches of our coastline are thus rendered unsuitable for alternative uses. In some cases the site itself may be geomorphologically unsuitable. It was pointed out in 1958 that the proposed site of the nuclear power station at Dungeness was on an eroding shoreline (Fig. 4.14). This was ignored, with the result that since construction almost constant beach nourishment of about 30,000m³ of pebbles per year has been required to reduce the threat of erosion of the site. The Thames estuary, Swansea Bay, Teesside, Humberside and the Firths of Forth and Clyde are all industrialised to some extent and now industrialisation has spread north to the more remote Cromarty Firth in Highland and Sullom Voe in Shetland.

The heavily canalised Mersey estuary is seriously polluted by urban and industrial waste. Even the open coast is not immune: the coast of Durham is polluted by colliery spoil and the Cumbrian coast boasts cliffs cut in industrial waste (Fig. 8.11). In 1984, about 30 per cent of all Britain's sewage sludge was dumped untreated into the sea and today the majority of British urban sewage outfalls still deliver raw, untreated sewage into the bathing zone. Many beaches in England and Wales still fail to reach EEC standards of cleanliness. Radioactive waste is also dumped into the sea from the nuclear reprocessing plant at Sellafield in Cumbria and although the concentrations were initially low, the build-up of potentially harmful radionucleides has been rapid. Add to this cocktail oil spills from large tanker accidents like *Amoco Cadiz*, *Christos Bitas* and *Eleni V* (all in 1978) and the oil swilled illegally from tankers washing out at sea, then it is not surprising that British coastal resorts are beginning to view the quality of their bathing water as a handicap. 'Eurobeaches' are expected to be clean. Government attitude in Britain so far has been to view our long coastline and strong tides as conducive to swift dispersal of pollutants. West Germany and the Netherlands, which have short coastlines and weak tides, take a

Fig. 8.12 Major components of a successful coastal zone management programme. Source: adapted from a South Carolina Coastal Council publicity leaflet.

1 BOUNDARIES OF THE COASTAL ZONE AND CRITICAL AREAS

2 INTERGOVERNMENT CO-ORDINATION

3 AREAS OF SPECIAL CONCERN FOR ECONOMIC, SOCIAL, HISTORICAL AND ENVIRONMENTAL REASONS

4 PUBLIC PARTICIPATION

5 PUBLIC BEACH ACCESS

6 BEACH EROSION CONTROL

7 MANAGEMENT OF MAJOR LAND AND WATER USES, INCLUDING THOSE OF REGIONAL AND NATIONAL INTEREST

8 MONITORING NEARSHORE WATERS FOR POLLUTION

9 ENVIRONMENTAL IMPACT STATEMENT CO-ORDINATION AND FUNDING

different view and have concentrated on efficient sewage treatment and reduction in pollution levels.

Strategies

Independent advances are being made on most of these fronts, yet the pollution of coastal water, the increasing demand for coastal space for housing, industry and recreation and problems of coastal erosion all have a common strand: they all relate to the coastal zone. As such their common solution lies in an integrated and co-ordinated approach to the coastal zone by governments. For example, in the United States, the Coastal Zone Management Act 1972 encouraged each coastal state to produce a management plan to cope with many of the problems noted above (Fig. 8.12). Beach erosion control was integrated with other land use considerations on a state-wide basis.

In Britain, some agencies do possess a coherent management plan. The Countryside Commission has designated 40 per cent of the undeveloped coast of England and Wales as 'Heritage Coast' and together with the Nature Conservancy Council advises local authorities on the management of coasts of high amenity or scientific value. The

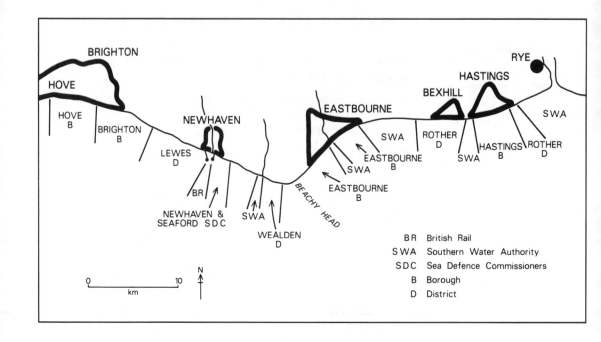

Fig. 8.13 shows map labels:

BRIGHTON
RYE
HASTINGS
HOVE
BEXHILL
EASTBOURNE
SWA
NEWHAVEN
HOVE B
ROTHER D
BRIGHTON B
SWA
LEWES D
EASTBOURNE B
BR
EASTBOURNE SWA
HASTINGS B
ROTHER D
SWA
NEWHAVEN & SEAFORD SDC
SWA
BEACHY HEAD
EASTBOURNE B
WEALDEN D

B R British Rail
S WA Southern Water Authority
S DC Sea Defence Commissioners
B Borough
D District

0 10 km
N

Fig. 8.13 The coastal protection responsibilities *alone* of this 64km stretch of East Sussex coast rests with no less than 10 authorities, each of which may legitimately pursue quite different coastal policies. This makes for difficulties in co-ordination (if any exists) in just this *one* realm of coastal management. Other responsibilities, such as land-use zoning, cliff-top planning, pollution control, provision of recreational facilities and wildlife and habitat protection may rest with yet more authorities along the same short stretch of coast. The result is coastal zone management in disarray.

Fig. 8.14 Without coastal zone management, is this the future of our coastline? (After a cartoon in the *Irish Times*.)

National Trust manages 14 per cent of the coast of England and Wales for the public benefit and, by virtue of its successful 'Enterprise Neptune' campaign, this figure is slowly rising. However, apart from the National Trust, most of the coast is primarily controlled by local authorities who may have no clear management plan for the coastal zone. This is not surprising since Britain does not possess in law a coastal zone as such: the seabed, the intertidal zone, the beach above high water mark and estuaries comprise the legal British coast. Different authorities have jurisdiction over each of these elements. Multiply this by the number of authorities *along* the coast and the management problems rocket (Fig. 8.13). Administrative boundaries are not geomorphological ones and many seawalls and groynes, for example, halt at the town boundary as adjacent authorities may pursue different policies towards the coast. Furthermore, cliff-top and other land use planning is currently controlled by town and country planning legislation, whereas coastal erosion is controlled by the Coast Protection Act 1949: issues of coastal dynamics are thus divorced from landward planning on the cliff top or backshore in spite of the common nature of the coastal system. Other countries have reacted to similar problems by declaring 'set-back' lines within which development is restricted. In Norway, the line is 100 m from the coastal edge; in Sweden it is 100–300 m inland.

As yet, Britain has neither the policies nor a coastal zone so defined and its management attempts have been piecemeal and unco-ordinated with no consistent long-term policy. There is a need for our coastline to be managed in a holistic and co-ordinated fashion, perhaps by a Coastal Commission with management powers extending from the coastal seas to a few hundred metres inland and responsibilities ranging from cliff-top and beach erosion to coastal pollution and recreation provision. The very future of our beautiful and varied coastline may be at stake (Fig. 8.14).

Sources and bibliography

There is a large and expanding literature relating to coastal processes and forms in addition to the rapidly increasing one concerned with the environmental and management aspects of the coast. Because of this, only a selection of fairly easily accessible material is given here. Included also are the source materials for the diagrams where appropriate.

General texts on coasts

Barnes, R.S.K. (1977) *The Coastline* (John Wiley, Chichester).
Bird, E.C.F. (1984) *Coasts* 3rd ed. (Basil Blackwell, Oxford).
Brunsden, D. and Doornkamp, J.C. (1972) *The Unquiet Landscape* pp. 71–100 (David and Charles, Newton Abbot).
Clayton, K.M. (1979) *Coastal Geomorphology* (Macmillan, London).
Davies, J.L. (1980) *Geographical Variation in Coastal Development* (Longman, London).
Davies, R.A. (1978) *Coastal Sedimentary Environments* (Springer-Verlag, New York).
King, C.A.M. (1972) *Beaches and Coasts* (Edward Arnold, London).
Komar, P.D. (1976) *Beach Processes and Sedimentation* (Prentice-Hall, Englewood Cliffs, New Jersey).
Pethick, J.S. (1984) *An Introduction to Coastal Geomorphology* (Edward Arnold, London).
Steers, J.A. (1946) *The Coastline of England and Wales* (Cambridge University Press, Cambridge).
Steers, J.A. (ed.) (1971) *Applied Coastal Geomorphology* (Macmillan, London).
Steers, J.A. (ed.) (1971) *Introduction to Coastline Development* (Macmillan, London).
Steers, J.A. (1973) *The Coastline of Scotland* (Cambridge University Press, Cambridge).

Further reading

In addition to the appropriate chapters in the texts mentioned above, the following books and articles may be of value in following up specific points. Most geographical and geological journals carry occasional articles on coasts; amongst these perhaps the most accessible are *Geography, Teaching Geography, Geographical Magazine, Journal of Geology, Field Studies, Progress in Physical Geography* and *Geography Review*. Some journals are specific to coastal or depositional environments; these include *Journal of Coastal Research, Marine Geology, Journal of Sedimentary Petrology, Shore and Beach, Coastal Zone Management Journal* and the *Journal of Shoreline Management*.

Chapter 1

Barnes, R.S.K. (1977) 'The Coastline', in Barnes, R.S.K. (ed.) *The Coastline* (John Wiley, Chichester).
Bloom, A.L. (1978) *Geomorphology* Chapter 20 (Prentice-Hall, New Jersey).
Bruun, P. (1971) 'Coastal research and its economic justification', in Steers, J.A. *Introduction to Coastline Development* (Macmillan, London).
Inman, D.L. and Brush, B.M. (1973) 'The coastal challenge', *Science* **181**, 20–31.
Jones, W.E. (1978) 'Keeping the sea at bay', *Sunday Times*, January 15.
Walker, H.J. (1978) 'Research in coastal geomorphology: basic and applied', in Embleton, C., Brunsden, D. and Jones, D.K.C. (eds) *Geomorphology* (Oxford University Press, Oxford).

Chapter 2

Clark, M. (1979) 'Marine processes', in Embleton, C. and Thornes, J. (eds) *Process in Geomorphology* (Edward Arnold, London).
Dugdale, R. (1981) 'Coastal processes', in Goudie, A. (ed.) *Geomorphological Techniques* (Allen and Unwin, London).
Gross, M.G. (1977) *Oceanography: a view of the earth,* Chapter 9 Tides and tidal currents (Prentice Hall, New Jersey).
Howarth, M.J. (1982) 'Tidal currents of the continental shelf', in Stride, A.H. (ed.) *Offshore Tidal Sands* (Chapman and Hall).
Judson, S. (1976) 'Erosion of the land: or what's happening to our continents?' in Tank, R.W. *Focus on Environmental Geology* (Oxford University Press, New York).
Komar, P.D. (1976) 'Nearshore currents and sediment transport and resulting beach configuration', in Stanley D.J. and Swift, D.J.P. (eds) *Marine Sediment Transport and Environmental Management* (Wiley, New York).
Lissau, S. (1977) 'Ocean waves', in Pirie, R.G. (ed.) *Oceanography* (Oxford University Press, New York).
M.A.F.F. (1981) *Atlas of the Seas around the British Isles* (Ministry of Agriculture, Fisheries and Food, H.M.S.O., London).

Milliman, J.D. and Meade, R.H. (1983) 'World-wide delivery of river sediment to the oceans', *Journal of Geology* **91**, 1–21.
Open University (1978) *Sediments*, Oceanography Unit II (Open University Press, Milton Keynes).
Open University (1978) *Ocean Water Movements*, Oceanography Unit 5 (Open University Press, Milton Keynes).
Trueman, A.E. (1971) *Geology and Scenery in England and Wales* (Penguin, Harmondsworth).
Whittow, J.B. (1974) *Geology and Scenery in Ireland* (Penguin, Harmondsworth).
Whittow, J.B. (1977) *Geology and Scenery in Scotland* (Penguin, Harmondsworth).

Chapter 3

Bridges, M. (1987) *Classic Landforms of the Gower Coast* (Geographical Association, Sheffield).
Brunsden, D. and Goudie, A.S. (1981) *Classic Coastal Landforms of Dorset* (Geographical Association, Sheffield).
Castleden, R. (1982) *Classic Landforms of the Sussex Coast* (Geographical Association, Sheffield).
Clark, M.J. and Small, R.J. (1982) *Slopes and Weathering* (Cambridge University Press, Cambridge).
Emery, K.O. and Kuhn, G.G. (1982) 'Sea cliffs; their processes, profiles and classification', *Geological Society of America Bulletin* **93**, 644–54.
Kean, P. (1986) *Classic Landforms of the North Devon Coast* (Geographical Association, Sheffield).
Mottershead, D.N. (1986) *Classic Landforms of the South Devon Coast* (Geographical Association, Sheffield).
Robinson, L.A. (1977) 'Marine erosive processes at the cliff foot', *Marine Geology* **23**, 257–71.
Sunamura, T. (1975) 'A laboratory study of wave cut platform formation', *Journal of Geology* **83**, 389–97.
Trenhaile, A.S. (1987) *The Geomorphology of Rock Coasts* (Oxford University Press, Oxford).
Trudgill, S.T. (1985) *Limestone Geomorphology,* Chapters 9 and 10 on Limestone coasts (Longman, Harlow).

Chapter 4

Allen, J.R. (1981) 'Beach erosion as a function of variation in the sediment budget, Sandy Hook, New Jersey, USA', *Earth Surface Processes and Landforms* **6,** 139–50.
Bascom, W.H. (1957) 'The relationship between sand size and beachface slope', *Transactions, American Geophysical Union* **33**, 866–74.
de Boer, G. (1964) 'Spurn Head, its history and evolution', *Transactions of the Institute of British Geographers* **34**, 71–89.
Brunsden, D. and Goudie, A.S. (1981) *Classic Coastal Landforms of Dorset* (Geographical Association, Sheffield).
Buchan, G. and Ritchie, W. (1979) 'Aberdeen Beach and Donmouth Spit: an example of short term coastal dynamics', *Scottish Geographical Magazine,* April, 27–43.
Carr, A.P. (1969) 'Size grading along a pebble beach', *Journal of Sedimentary Petrology* **39**(1), 297–311.
Carr, A.P. (1972) 'Aspects of spit development and decay: the estuary of the Rive Ore, Suffolk', *Field Studies* 3(4), 633–53.
Clayton, K.M. (1980) 'Beach sediment budgets and coastal modification', *Progress in Physical Geography* **4**(4), 471–87.
Davies, J.L. (1974) 'The coastal sediment compartment', *Australian Geographical Studies* **12,** 139–61.
Davis, R.A. (1978) 'Beach and nearshore zone', in Davis, R.A. (ed.) *Coastal Sedimentary Environments* (Springer-Verlag, New York).
Hayes, M.O. (1967) 'Relationship between coastal climate and bottom sediment type on the inner continental shelf', *Marine Geology* **5**, 111–32.
Randell, R.E. (1977) 'Shingle Street and the sea', *Geographical Magazine* **9,** 569–73.
Wright, L.D. (1978) 'River deltas', in Davis, R.A. (ed.) *Coastal Sedimentary Environments* (Springer-Verlag, New York).
Wright, L.D. and Coleman, J.M. (1972) 'River delta morphology: wave climate and the role of the subaqueous profile', *Science* **176,** 282–89.

Chapter 5

Boorman, L.A. (1971) 'Sand dunes', in Barnes, R.S.K. (ed.) *The Coastline* (Wiley, New York)
Chapman, V.J. (1976) *Coastal Vegetation* (Pergamon, Oxford).

Goldsmith, V. (1978) 'Coastal dunes', in Davis, R.A. (ed.) *Coastal Sedimentary Environments* (Springer-Verlag, New York).

Landsberg, S.Y. (1956) 'The orientation of dunes in Britain and Denmark in relation to wind', *Geographical Journal* 112(1), 176–89.

Mather, A.S. and Ritchie, W. (1977) *The Beaches of the Highlands and Islands of Scotland* (Countryside Commission for Scotland, Perth).

Pye, K. (1983) 'Coastal dunes', *Progress in Physical Geography* 7(4), 531–57.

Ritchie, W. (1972) 'The evolution of coastal dunes', *Scottish Geographical Magazine* 88, 19, 35.

Chapter 6

Beeftink, W.G. (1977) 'Salt-marshes', in Barnes, R.S.K. (ed.) *The Coastline* (Wiley, New York).

Frey, R.W. and Bason, P.B. (1978) 'Coastal salt marshes', in Davis, R.A. (ed.) *Coastal Sedimentary Environments* (Springer-Verlag, New York).

Gresswell, R.K. (1964) 'The origin of the Mersey and Dee estuaries', *Geological Journal* 4(1), 77–86.

Robinson, A.H.W. (1960) 'Ebb-flood channel systems in sandy bays and estuaries', *Geography* 45, 183–91.

Chapter 7

Curray, J.R. (1964) 'Transgression and regression', in Mills, R.L. (ed.) *Papers in Marine Geology:* Shepard Commemorative Volume (Macmillan, London).

Dawson, A.G. (1980) 'Shore erosion by frost: an example from the Scottish Lateglacial', in Lowe, J.J., Gray, J.M. and Robinson, J.E. (eds) *Studies in the Lateglacial of North West Europe* (Pergamon, Oxford).

Evans, G. (1979) 'Quaternary transgression and regression', *Journal of the Geological Society of London* 136, 125–32.

Goudie, A.S. (1983) *Environmental Change* (Oxford University Press, Oxford).

Kidson, C. (1982) 'Sea-level changes in the Holocene', *Quaternary Science Reviews* 1(2), 121–51.

Mitchell, F. (1976) *The Irish Landscape* (Collins, London).

Chapter 8

Carter, R.W.G. (1980) 'Human activity and geomorphic processes: the example of recreational pressure on the Northern Ireland coast', *Zeitschrift für Geomorphologie*, N.F. 34, 155–64.

Clark, M.J. (1974) 'Conflict on the coast', *Geography* 59, 93–103.

Clark, M.J. (1978) 'Geomorphology in coastal zone environmental management', *Geography*, 63, 273–83.

Clark, M.J., Ricketts, P.J. and Small, R.J. (1976) 'Barton does not rule the waves', *Geographical Magazine* 48, 580–88.

Clayton, K. (1977) 'Salvation from the sea', *Geographical Magazine* 10, 622–25.

Commission of European Communities (1987) *The State of the Environment in the European Community, 1986* (Office for Publications of the European Communities, Luxembourg).

Corney, G. (1987) 'Question and answer: Coastal Management, 1984', *Geography Review* 1(1), 29–32.

Greenpeace (1987) *Coastline, Britain's Threatened Heritage* (Kingfisher Books, London).

Gribbon, J. (1984) 'The world's beaches are vanishing', *New Scientist* May 10, 30–32.

Hails, J.R. (1977) 'Geomorphology in coastal zone planning and management', in Hails, J.R. (ed.) *Applied Geomorphology* (Elsevier).

H.M.S.O. (1911) *Royal Commission on Coastal Erosion,* Report (Her Majesty's Stationery Office, London).

Jolliffe, I.P. (1983) 'Coastal erosion and flooding: what are the broad options?' *Geographical Journal* 149(1), 62–67.

Ritchie, W. (1981) 'Where land meets the sea', *Geographical Magazine,* September, 772–74.

Robinson, A.H.W. (1980) 'Erosion and accretion along part of the Suffolk coast of East Anglia, England', *Marine Geology* 37, 133–46.

Rosenbaum, J.G. (1976) 'Shoreline structures as a cause of shoreline erosion: A review', in Tank, R.W. *Focus on Environmental Geology* (Oxford University Press, New York).

Schools Council (1984) *Coastal Management*, A case study of Barton-on-Sea, Geography 16–19 (Schools Council Publications. Longman Resources Unit, York).

South Carolina Coastal Council (1978) Coastal management publicity leaflet (Office of Coastal Planning, Charleston, South Carolina).

Wood, A. (1978) 'Coast erosion at Aberystwyth, the geological and human factors involved', *Geological Journal* 13(1), 61–72.

Index